The Practise of English Language Teaching

The Practise of English Language Teaching

Mrinal K Ghosh

AUTHORSPRESS

Worldwide Circulation through Authorspress Global Network
First Published 2009
by
Authorspress
E-35/103, Jawahar Park
Laxmi Nagar, Delhi-110 092
e-mail: authorspress@yahoo.com

The Practise of English Language Teaching
ISBN 978-81-7273-491-6

Printed in India at Tarun Offset, Delhi.

Preface

With English becoming the *lingua franca* of the new globalised world, English language teaching has assumed new proportions in this day and age. With the insistence on English teaching becoming ever more pressing and essential, English language teaching has come about to assume ever greater proportions. The practice of English teaching today has to not only take into account the rigours of traditional teaching practices, but also focus on the more critical daily use aspects of the field, which make English so important in today's world.

The present text as been designed as a manual which looks into the practice of teaching English language today. The text seeks to give readers a broad insight into the methodologies, practices and processes which enable English language teaching, and acquaints readers with the current trends and developments in the field. Focusing on the rigours of the pedagogical challenges, the text seeks to give readers a panoramic look into the what gives the field its importance, and how to go about the issues and problems that crop up in its wake. With case studies and situational examples incorporated, the text serves to bring pragmatic insights into the text.

It is hoped that the insight and erudition of the text serves well for all. Any suggestions for further improvement are most welcome.

Mrinal K Ghosh

Contents

1

Introduction to English Language

1.1. History of English Language

English belongs to the Indo-European family of languages. Within this family, English is a member of the Germanic branch. The Germanic branch may be divided into three groups or subdivisions: East Germanic which consisted of Gothic, now an extinct language; North Germanic under which we include the Scandinavian languages; and West Germanic which consists of High German, Low German, Frisian and English.

Three tribes settled in England. These were the Angles, the Jutes, and the Saxons. The Angles came from Denmark, the Saxons were from Holstein in the south, and the Jutes were from the north. These and the Frisian were worshippers of Ing. Linguistic and religious associations between these tribes resulted in a bundle of related dialects, which we presently call English.

English is a member of the Indo-European family of languages. This broad family includes most of the European languages spoken today. The Indo-European family includes several major branches: Latin and the modern Romance languages (French etc.); the Germanic languages (English, German, Swedish etc.); the Indo-Iranian languages (Hindi, Urdu, Sanskrit etc.); the Slavic languages (Russian, Polish, Czech etc.); the Baltic languages of Latvian and Lithuanian; the Celtic languages (Welsh, Irish Gaelic etc.); Greek.

The influence of the original Indo-European language can be seen today, even though no written record of it exists. The word for *father*, for example, is *vater* in German, *pater* in Latin, and *pitr* in Sanskrit. These words are all cognates, similar words in different languages that share the same root.

Of these branches of the Indo-European family, two are, as far as the study of the development of English is concerned, of paramount importance, the Germanic and the Romance. English is a member of the Germanic group of languages. It is believed that this group began as a common language in the Elbe river region about 3,000 years ago. By the second century BC, this Common Germanic language had split into three distinct sub-groups:

– East Germanic was spoken by peoples who migrated back to southeastern Europe. No East Germanic language is spoken today, and the only written East Germanic language that survives is Gothic.
– North Germanic evolved into the modern Scandinavian languages of Swedish, Danish, Norwegian, and Icelandic.
– West Germanic is the ancestor of modern German, Dutch, Flemish, Frisian, and English.

1.1.1. Old English (500-1100 AD)

West Germanic invaders from Jutland and southern Denmark: the Angles, Saxons, and Jutes, began to settle in the British Isles in the fifth and sixth centuries AD. They spoke a mutually intelligible language, similar to modern Frisian—the language of the northeastern region of the Netherlands—that is called Old English. Four major dialects of Old English emerged, Northumbrian in the north of England, Mercian in the Midlands, West Saxon in the south and west, and Kentish in the Southeast. These invaders pushed the original, Celtic-speaking inhabitants out of what is now England into Scotland, Wales, Cornwall, and Ireland, leaving behind a few Celtic words. These Celtic languages survive today in the Gaelic languages of Scotland and Ireland and in Welsh. Cornish, unfortunately, is, in linguistic terms, now a dead language. Also influencing English at this time were the Vikings. Norse invasions and settlement, beginning around 850, brought many North Germanic words into the language, particularly in the north of England. Some examples are *dream*, which had meant 'joy' until the Vikings imparted its current meaning on it from the Scandinavian cognate *draumr*, and *skirt*, which continues to live alongside its native English cognate *shirt*.

The majority of words in modern English come from foreign, not Old English roots. In fact, only about one sixth of the known Old English words have descendants surviving today. But this is deceptive; Old English is much more important than these statistics would indicate. About half of the most commonly used words in modern English have Old English roots. Words like *be*, *water*, and *strong*, for example, derive from Old English roots.

1.1.2. Middle English (1100-1500)

William the Conqueror, the Duke of Normandy, invaded and conquered England and the Anglo-Saxons in 1066 AD. The new overlords spoke a dialect of Old French known as Anglo-Norman. The Normans were also of Germanic stock and Anglo-Norman was a French dialect that had considerable Germanic influences in addition to the basic Latin roots.

Prior to the Norman Conquest, Latin had been only a minor influence on the English language, mainly through vestiges of the Roman occupation and from the conversion of Britain to Christianity in the seventh century, but now there was a wholesale infusion of Romance (Anglo-Norman) words.

The influence of the Normans can be illustrated by looking at two words, beef and cow. *Beef*, commonly eaten by the aristocracy, derives from the Anglo-Norman, while the Anglo-Saxon commoners, who tended the cattle, retained the Germanic *cow*. Many legal terms, such as *indict*, *jury* , and *verdict* have Anglo-Norman roots because the Normans ran the courts. This split, where words commonly used by the aristocracy have Romantic roots and words frequently used by the Anglo-Saxon commoners have Germanic roots, can be seen in many instances.

Sometimes French words replaced Old English words; *crime* replaced *firen* and *uncle* replaced *eam*. Other times, French and Old English components combined to form a new word, as the French *gentle* and the Germanic *man* formed *gentleman*. Other times, two different words with roughly the same meaning survive into modern English. Thus we have the Germanic *doom* and the French *judgment*, or *wish* and *desire*.

In 1204 AD, King John lost the province of Normandy to the King of France. This began a process where the Norman nobles of England became increasingly estranged from their French cousins. England became the chief concern of the nobility, rather than their estates in France, and consequently the nobility adopted a modified English as their native tongue. About 150 years later, the Black Death (1349-50) killed about one third of the English population. And as a result of this the labouring and merchant classes grew in economic and social importance, and along with them English increased in importance compared to Anglo-Norman.

This mixture of the two languages came to be known as Middle English. The most famous example of Middle English is *Chaucer's Canterbury Tales.* Unlike Old English, Middle English can be read, albeit with difficulty, by modern English-speaking people. By 1362, the linguistic division between the nobility and the commoners was largely over. In that year, the Statute of Pleading was adopted, which made English the language of the courts and it began to be used in Parliament.

1.1.3. Early Modern English (1500-1800)

The revival of classical scholarship brought many classical Latin and Greek words into the Language. These borrowings were deliberate and many bemoaned the adoption of these "inkhorn" terms, but many survive to this day. Shakespeare's character Holofernes in *Loves Labor Lost* is a satire of an overenthusiastic schoolmaster who is too fond of Latinisms.

Many students having difficulty understanding *Shakespeare* would be surprised to learn that he wrote in modern English. But, as can be seen in the earlier example of the Lord's Prayer, Elizabethan English has much more in common with our language today than it does with the language of Chaucer. Many familiar words and phrases were coined or first recorded by Shakespeare, some 2,000 words and countless idioms are his. Newcomers to Shakespeare are often shocked at the number of cliches contained in his plays, until they realise that he coined them and they became cliches afterwards. "One fell swoop," "vanish into thin air," and "flesh and blood" are all Shakespeare's.

Two other major factors influenced the language and served to separate Middle and Modern English. The first was the Great Vowel Shift. This was a change in pronunciation that began around 1400. While modern English speakers can read Chaucer with some difficulty, Chaucer's pronunciation would have been completely unintelligible to the modern ear. Shakespeare, on the other hand, would be accented, but understandable. Vowel sounds began to be made further to the front of the mouth and the letter "e" at the end of words became silent. Chaucer's *Lyf* became the modern *life*. In Middle English *name* was pronounced "nam-a," *five* was pronounced "feef," and *down* was pronounced "doon." In linguistic terms, the shift was rather sudden, the major changes occurring within a century. The shift is still not over, however, vowel sounds are still shortening although the change has become considerably more gradual.

The last major factor in the development of Modern English was the advent of the printing press. William Caxton brought the printing press to England in 1476. Books became cheaper and as a result, literacy became more common. Publishing for the masses became a profitable enterprise, and works in English, as opposed to Latin, became more common. Finally, the printing press brought standardisation to English. The dialect of London, where most publishing houses were located, became the standard. Spelling and grammar became fixed, and the first English dictionary was published in 1604.

1.1.4. Late-Modern English (1800-Present)

The principal distinction between early- and late-modern English is vocabulary. Pronunciation, grammar, and spelling are largely the same, but Late-Modern English has many more words. These words are the result of two historical factors. The first is the Industrial Revolution and the rise of the technological society. This necessitated new words for things and ideas that had not previously existed. The second was the British Empire. At its height, Britain ruled one quarter of the earth's surface, and English adopted many foreign words and made them its own.

The industrial and scientific revolutions created a need for neologisms to describe the new creations and discoveries. For this, English relied heavily on Latin and Greek. Words like *oxygen, protein, nuclear,* and *vaccine* did not exist in the classical languages, but they were created from Latin and Greek roots. Such neologisms were not exclusively created from classical roots though, English roots were used for such terms as *horsepower, airplane*, and *typewriter*. This burst of neologisms continues today, perhaps most visible in the field of electronics and computers. *Byte, cyber-, bios, hard-drive,* and *microchip* are good examples.

Also, the rise of the British Empire and the growth of global trade served not only to introduce English to the world, but to introduce words into English. Hindi, and the other languages of the Indian subcontinent, provided many words, such as *pundit, shampoo, pajamas,* and *juggernaut*. Virtually every language on Earth has contributed to the development of English, from Finnish (*sauna*) and Japanese (*tycoon*) to the vast contributions of French and Latin.

Finally, the military influence on the language during the latter half of twentieth century was significant. Before the Great War, military service for English-speaking persons was rare; both Britain and the United States maintained small, volunteer militaries. Military slang existed, but with the exception of nautical terms, rarely influenced standard English. During the mid-20th century, however, a large number of British and American men served in the military. And consequently military slang entered the language like never before. *Blockbuster, nose dive, camouflage, radar, roadblock, spearhead,* and *landing strip* are all military terms that made their way into standard English.

1.1.5. American English

Also significant beginning around 1600 AD was the English colonisation of North America and the subsequent creation of American English. Some pronunciations and usages "froze" when they reached the American shore. In certain respects, some varieties of American English are closer to the English of Shakespeare than modern Standard English is. Some "Americanisms" are actually originally English English expressions that were preserved in the colonies while lost at home.

The American dialect also served as the route of introduction for many native American words into the English language. Most often, these were place names like *Mississippi, Roanoke,* and *Iowa*. Indian-sounding names like *Idaho* were sometimes created that had no native-American roots. But, names for other things besides places were also common. *Raccoon, tomato, canoe, barbecue, savanna,* and *hickory* have native American roots, although in many cases the original Indian words were mangled almost beyond recognition.

Spanish has also been great influence on American English. M*ustang, canyon, ranch, stampede,* and *vigilante* are all examples of Spanish words that made their way into English through the settlement of the American West.

A lesser number of words have entered American English from French and West African languages.

Likewise dialects of English have developed in many of the former colonies of the British Empire. There are distinct forms of the English language spoken in Australia, New Zealand, South Africa, India and many other parts of the world.

1.1.6. Chronology of the English Language

449	Anglo-Saxon settlement of Britain begins
450-480	Earliest Old English inscriptions date from this period
597	St. Augustine arrives in Britain. Beginning of Christian conversion
731	The Venerable Bede publishes The Ecclesiastical History of the English People in Latin
792	Viking raids and settlements begin
871	Alfred becomes king of Wessex. He has Latin works translated into English and begins practice of English prose. The Anglo-Saxon Chronicle is begun
911	Charles II of France grants Normandy to the Viking chief Hrolf the Ganger. The beginning of Norman French
c. 1000	The oldest surviving manuscript of Beowulf dates from this period
1066	The Norman conquest
c. 1150	The oldest surviving manuscripts of Middle English date from this period
1171	Henry II conquers Ireland
1204	King John loses the province of Normandy to France

1348	English replaces Latin as the medium of instruction in schools, other than Oxford and Cambridge which retain Latin
1362	The Statute of Pleading replaces French with English as the language of law. Records continue to be kept in Latin. English is used in Parliament for the first time
1384	Wyclif publishes his English translation of the Bible
c. 1388	Chaucer begins The Canterbury Tales
1476	William Caxton establishes the first English printing press
1492	Columbus discovers the New World
1549	First version of The Book of Common Prayer
1604	Robert Cawdrey publishes the first English dictionary, Table Alphabeticall
1607	Jamestown, the first permanent English settlement in the New World, established
1611	The Authorised, or King James Version, of the Bible is published
1702	Publication of the first daily, English-language newspaper, The Daily Courant, in London
1755	Samuel Johnson publishes his dictionary
1770	Cook discovers Australia
1928	The Oxford English Dictionary is published

Modern English presents a peculiar picture. It has retained the old spelling, even as it developed new pronunciation – modern pronunciation with medieval spelling. Many Latin words were borrowed into English through French. This period also saw development of regularity in vocabulary, in form and usage, grammatical forms, and in syntax.

English language developed a tendency and respect for correctness in the Seventeenth Century. "Accessions to the vocabulary in the 17th Century show the influence of French and Italian, particularly in matters of fashion and the fine arts. The 18th Century showed the influence of more distant countries such as India, and the 19th Century continued that tendency. However, scientific terms are the outstanding contribution of the 19th

Century, and this has remained true in the 20th" (*Encyclopedia Britannica*).

1.2. Characteristics of English Language

1.2.1. Receptivity to Loan Words

An important characteristic of English has been its receptivity to loan words from other languages. No other language exhibits such an extraordinary receptivity. This has not resulted, however, in the loss of corresponding native words in most cases. Words were often borrowed to refine the meanings which resulted in greater clarity in the expression and creation of ideas. Moreover, English speakers always enjoyed greater freedom in the use of their language, unlike, for instance, the users of the French language. There has been no legal provision which guided the native speakers of English in the use or non-use of words. Mostly the commonly agreed conventions, rather than deliberate enforcement of rules of usage through academies, marked the development of English and its use.

Modern, current English has over 500,000 words. If we add the scientific terms used in the language, the total would be very high indeed. It has been estimated that only 18.4 per cent of these words is native to English. French vocabulary used in English is around 32.4 per cent, whereas the words of Latin origin is estimated to be 14.4 per cent, words of Greek origin around 12.5 per cent, and other languages 23.3 per cent. This does not mean that the words of foreign origin are more greatly used in English. It only suggests that more foreign words than the native ones are used to characterise, define, and describe meanings and ideas in English.

1.2.2. English Dialects

Two principal branches of spoken English dialects are recognised by scholars. The British branch of spoken dialects include those spoken in England, Ireland, Wales, Scotland, Australia, New Zealand, and South Africa. The North American branch of spoken dialects include those spoken in Canada and the United States. Within each of these categories, there are different dialects, both geographical and social.

The English spoken in the Eastern Seaboard region and adjoining states in the United States have been studied in greater detail than the English spoken in other parts of the United States. Generally speaking, there are three different dialect areas: Northern dialect area consisting of Maine, New Hampshire, Rhode Island, and eastern Massachusetts and Connecticut; the Midland dialect area consisting of Pennsylvania, southern New Jersey, northern Maryland, and northern West Virginia is treated as North Midland dialect; and the area consisting of West Virginia, western Virginia, western North Carolina, and northwestern South Carolina is treated as South Midland. The Southern English dialect includes Delmarva, Virginia Piedmont, Northeastern North Carolina, Cape Fear and Peedee Valleys and the South Carolina country.

It is possible that these three major dialect areas in the eastern United States extend to the west in close conjunction with the history of westward movement in settlement in the U.S. However, as Gleason warned us years ago, it is only "American folk-linguistics (which) recognises two major dialect areas, 'Southern' and 'Northern.' But there is no discernible linguistic division at or near the Mason-Dixon line. 'Southern' dialects are exceedingly diverse. The sharpest dialect boundary in the United States runs directly through the South roughly along the Blue Ridge mountains. A 'Northern dialect' is as much a fiction as a 'Southern dialect.'" Despite spoken dialectal differences, the native speakers of English have maintained a great uniformity in formal spoken English which is amazingly uniform and close to written English. An educated native speaker of English makes easy transitions from the colloquial/informal to varieties of formal English in his/her speech.

The teacher of TESOL (Teaching English to Speakers of Other Languages), who is a native of speaker of English, needs to give up the peculiarities of his/her regional and/or social dialect at the informal level, and to switch over to the standard which is closer to the ordinary, plain written English, in his/her classroom.

1.2.3. Spelling

Modern English has retained the old spelling even as it has developed new pronunciation. English is rather "notorious" for its alleged frequent lack of correspondence between the spelling and pronunciation of a word. It has been pointed out that "there are 13.7 spellings per sound, but only 3.5 sounds per letter" in English.

Contrary to general impression, scholars claim that 75% of English is regular. However, "the 400 or so irregular spellings are largely among the most frequently used words in the language, and this promotes a strong impression of irregularity". Irregularities of English spelling came from several sources into the language. 26 letters are used to represent a larger number of phonemes. Borrowed words from French led to respelling of words. The printing process caused further complications. Many early printers were from Holland and they introduced their own spelling norms, and made several convenient abbreviations and additions and deletions to account for the space in a line. Then "there was a fashion to make spelling reflect Latin or Greek etymology." And modern borrowings from other languages brought with them their own spelling. In spite of all this, English spelling gives us a lot of information about the relationship between words. And this feature is a boon both to the TESOL teacher, and the second/foreign language learner of English. One comes to recognise intuitively the relationship between words, learns to derive the nouns from the verbs and vice versa, and does a lot of other grammatical exercises which make the learning of English much simpler than learning many other languages.

English has a long history of spelling reform movements from the 16th Century. The efforts of Spelling Reform Association in the U.S. and Simplified Spelling Society in Britain, along with the untiring efforts of Bernard Shaw, a great modern playwright, in recent times, are significant milestones in spelling reform movements. But almost all of these ended as futile exercise. However, some spelling changes have been effected in American English through the rules introduced by the great American lexicographer Noah Webster which distinguish American English from British English. For example, use of -or for -our and -er for -re in words such as honor/honour, and theater/theatre.

1.2.4. Grammar

English grammar has minimal inflection compared with most

other Indo-European languages. For example, Modern English, unlike Modern German or Dutch and the Romance languages, lacks grammatical gender and adjectival agreement. Case marking has almost disappeared from the language and mainly survives in pronouns. The patterning of strong (e.g. speak/spoke/spoken) versus weak verbs inherited from its Germanic origins has declined in importance in modern English, and the remnants of inflection (such as plural marking) have become more regular. At the same time, the language has become more analytic, and has developed features such as modal verbs and word order as resources for conveying meaning. Auxiliary verbs mark constructions such as questions, negative polarity, the passive voice and progressive aspect.

1.2.5. Vocabulary

The English vocabulary has changed considerably over the centuries. Like many languages deriving from *Proto-Indo-European* (PIE), many of the most common words in English can trace back their origin (through the Germanic branch) to PIE. Such words include the basic pronouns *I*, from Old English ic, (cf. Latin *ego*, Greek *ego*, Sanskrit *aham*), *me* (cf. Latin *me*, Greek *eme*, Sanskrit *mam*), numbers (e.g. *one, two, three*, cf. Latin *unus, duo, tres*, Greek *oinos* "ace (on dice)", *duo, treis*), common family relationships such as mother, father, brother, sister etc (cf. Greek "meter", Latin "mater", Sanskrit "mat?"; *mother*), names of many animals (cf. Sankrit *mus*, Greek *mys*, Latin *mus*; *mouse*), and many common verbs (cf. Greek *gignômi*, Latin *gnoscere*, Hittite *kanes*; *to know*).

Germanic words tend to be shorter than the Latinate words of English and more common in ordinary speech. This includes nearly all the basic pronouns, prepositions, conjunctions, modal verbs etc. that form the basis of English syntax and grammar. The longer Latinate words are often regarded as more elegant or educated. However, the excessive use of Latinate words is considered at times to be either pretentious or an attempt to obfuscate an issue. George Orwell's essay "Politics and the English Language", considered an important scrutinisation of the English language, is critical of this, as well as other perceived misuse of the language.

An English speaker is in many cases able to choose between Germanic and Latinate synonyms: *come* or *arrive; sight* or *vision; freedom* or *liberty*. In some cases, there is a choice between a Germanic derived word (*oversee*), a Latin derived word (*supervise*), and a French word derived from the same Latin word (*survey*). Such synonyms harbor a variety of different meanings and nuances, enabling the speaker to express fine variations or shades of thought. Familiarity with the of groups of synonyms can give English speakers greater control over their linguistic register.

An exception to this and a peculiarity perhaps unique to English is that the nouns for meats are commonly different from, and unrelated to, those for the animals from which they are produced, the animal commonly having a Germanic name and the meat having a French-derived one. Examples include: deer and venison; cow and beef; *swine*/pig and pork, or sheep and mutton. This is assumed to be a result of the aftermath of the Norman invasion, where a French-speaking elite were the consumers of the meat, produced by Anglo-Saxon lower classes.

Since the majority of words used in informal settings will normally be Germanic, such words are often the preferred choices when a speaker wishes to make a point in an argument in a very direct way. A majority of Latinate words (or at least a majority of content words) will normally be used in more formal speech and writing, such as a courtroom or an encyclopedia article. However, there are other Latinate words that are used normally in everyday speech and do not sound formal; these are mainly words for concepts that no longer have Germanic words, and are generally assimilated better and in many cases do not appear Latinate. For instance, the words *mountain, valley, river, aunt, uncle, move, use, push* and *stay* are all Latinate.

English easily accepts technical terms into common usage and often imports new words and phrases. Examples of this phenomenon include: cookie, Internet and URL (technical terms), as well as genre, über, lingua franca and *amigo* (imported words/ phrases from French, German, modern Latin, and Spanish, respectively). In addition, slang often provides new meanings for old words and phrases. In fact, this fluidity is so pronounced that a distinction often needs to be made between formal forms of English and contemporary usage.

1.2.6. Number of words in English

The vocabulary of English is undoubtedly vast, but assigning a specific number to its size is more a matter of definition than of calculation. Unlike other languages, such as French, German, Spanish and Italian there is no Academy to define officially accepted words and spellings. Neologisms are coined regularly in medicine, science and technology and other fields, and new slang is constantly developed. Some of these new words enter wide usage; others remain restricted to small circles. Foreign words used in immigrant communities often make their way into wider English usage. Archaic, dialectal, and regional words might or might not be widely considered as "English".

1.2.7. Writing System

English has been written using the Latin alphabet since around the ninth century. (Before that, Old English had been written using Anglo-Saxon runes.) The spelling system, or orthography, is multilayered, with elements of French, Latin and Greek spelling on top of the native Germanic system; it has grown to vary significantly from the phonology of the language. The spelling of words often diverges considerably from how they are spoken.

Though letters and sounds may not correspond in isolation, spelling rules that take into account syllable structure, phonetics, and accents are 75% or more reliable. Some phonics spelling advocates claim that English is more than 80% phonetic. In general, the English language, being the product of many other languages and having only been codified orthographically in the 16th century, has fewer consistent relationships between sounds and letters than many other languages. The consequence of this orthographic history is that reading can be challenging. It takes longer for students to become completely fluent readers of English than of many other languages, including French, Greek, and Spanish.

Unlike most other Germanic languages, English has almost no diacritics except in foreign loanwords (like the acute accent in *café*), and in the uncommon use of a diaeresis mark (often in formal writing) to indicate that two vowels are pronounced separately, rather than as one sound. It may be acceptable to leave out the marks, depending on the target audience, or the context in which the word is used.

Some English words retain the diacritic to distinguish them from others, such as animé, exposé, lamé, öre, øre, pâté, piqué, and rosé, though these are sometimes also dropped (résumé/*resumé* is usually spelled *resume* in the United States). There are loan words which occasionally use a diacritic to represent their pronunciation that is not in the original word, such as *maté*, from Spanish yerba mate, following the French usage, but they are extremely rare.

A version of the language almost universally agreed upon by educated English speakers around the world is called formal written English. It takes virtually the same form no matter where in the English-speaking world it is written. In spoken English, by contrast, there are a vast number of differences between dialects, accents, and varieties of slang, colloquial and regional expressions. In spite of this, local variations in the formal written version of the language are quite limited, being restricted largely to the spelling differences between British and American English.

1.2.8. Simplified Versions

To make English easier to read, there are some simplified versions of the language. One basic version is named Basic English, a constructed language with a small number of words created by Charles Kay Ogden and described in his book *Basic English: A General Introduction with Rules and Grammar*. The language is based on a simplified version of English. Ogden said that it would take seven years to learn English, seven months for Esperanto, and seven weeks for Basic English, comparable with Ido. Thus companies who need to make complex books for international use employ Basic English, and by language schools that need to give people some knowledge of English in a short time.

Ogden did not put any words into Basic English that could be said with a few other words and he worked to make the words work for speakers of any other language. He put his set of words through a large number of tests and adjustments. He also made the grammar simpler, but tried to keep the grammar normal for English users. The concept gained its greatest publicity just after the Second World War as a tool for world peace. Although it was not built into a programme, similar simplifications were devised for various international uses.

Another version, Simplified English, exists, which is a controlled language originally developed for aerospace industry maintenance manuals. It offers a carefully limited and standardised subset of English. Simplified English has a lexicon of approved words and those words can only be used in certain ways. For example, the word *close* can be used in the phrase "Close the door" but not "do not go close to the landing gear".

1.2.9. Plain English

Of great interest and relevance to the teacher of TESOL are the on-going movements against the unnecessarily complicated use of English and for the replacement of such usage by clearer forms of expression. Both in Britain and the United States, because of pressure from teachers, authors, writers and communicators, governments have made efforts to redesign forms and reports, etc., in plain English which could be understood with ease.

President Carter issued an Executive Order in March 1978 requiring regulations to be written in plain English. This order was revoked by President Reagan in 1981, but "it promoted a great deal of legislation throughout the country, and an increase in plain English usage among corporations".

As a consequence of growing interest in Plain English, instruction manuals, government forms and documents, and many other materials for public use have been greatly simplified. Medical labels, Nutrition Facts, etc., are presented in readable and easily understandable form. Corporations have begun to use the services of skilled technical literature writers for this purpose. There has, however, been continued objection from legal professions based on "the risk of ambiguity inherent in the use of every day language" which, they claim, makes it unsuitable for precision.

The following are the characteristics of Plain English:

1. Prefer the shorter word to the longer one.
2. Use simple, everyday words rather than fancy ones.
3. Prefer verbs over nouns and adjectives.
4. Prefer the specific word to the general.
5. Write short sentences with an average of no more than 20 words.

6. Use the active voice rather than the passive.
7. Be a miser with compound and complex sentences and a spend thrift with simple sentences.
8. Write short paragraphs with an average of about 765 words.
9. Avoid paragraphs that exceed five typed lines for business letters and ten lines for longer compositions.
10. Write with the ear. A sentence may look good on paper but its cadence may be jarring. Listen to your sentences in your head as you write, and do not write anything that you could not comfortably say.
11. Write for the eye as well as the mind. Prepare an overall design, positioning understandable headings, subheadings, and captions for each segment, showing the organisation of the text. Make the whole document visually appealing.
12. Use appropriate underlining, ink color that contrasts sharply with the paper, lists, boxes or panels, bold or other typefaces to emphasize points.
13. Use 'white space' in margins, between sections, paragraphs, and lines to make the document look good.

1.3. Geographical Distribution of English

Approximately 375 million people speak English as their first language. English today is probably the third largest language by number of native speakers, after Mandarin Chinese and Spanish. However, when combining native and non-native speakers it is probably the most commonly spoken language in the world, though possibly second to a combination of the Chinese languages, depending on whether or not distinctions in the latter are classified as "languages" or "dialects." Estimates that include second language speakers vary greatly from 470 million to over a billion depending on how literacy or mastery is defined. There are some who claim that non-native speakers now outnumber native speakers by a ratio of 3 to 1.

The countries with the highest populations of native English speakers are, in descending order: United States (215 million), United Kingdom (58 million), Canada (18.2 million), Australia

(15.5 million), Ireland (3.8 million), South Africa (3.7 million), and New Zealand (3.0-3.7 million). Countries such as Jamaica and Nigeria also have millions of native speakers of dialect continua ranging from an English-based creole to a more standard version of English. Of those nations where English is spoken as a second language, India has the most such speakers ('Indian English') and linguistics professor David Crystal claims that, combining native and non-native speakers, India now has more people who speak or understand English than any other country in the world.

English is the primary language in Anguilla, Antigua and Barbuda, Australia (Australian English), the Bahamas, Barbados, Bermuda, Belize (Belizean Kriol), the British Indian Ocean Territory, the British Virgin Islands, Canada (Canadian English), the Cayman Islands, the Falkland Islands, Gibraltar, Grenada, Guam, Guernsey (Channel Island English), Guyana, Ireland (Hiberno-English), Isle of Man (Manx English), Jamaica (Jamaican English), Jersey, Montserrat, Nauru, New Zealand (New Zealand English), Pitcairn Islands, Saint Helena, Saint Kitts and Nevis, Saint Vincent and the Grenadines, Singapore, South Georgia and the South Sandwich Islands, Trinidad and Tobago, the Turks and Caicos Islands, the United Kingdom, the U.S. Virgin Islands, and the United States.

In many other countries, where English is not the most spoken language, it is an official language; these countries include Botswana, Cameroon, Dominica, Fiji, the Federated States of Micronesia, Ghana, Gambia, India, Kenya, Kiribati, Lesotho, Liberia, Madagascar, Malta, the Marshall Islands, Mauritius, Namibia, Nigeria, Pakistan, Palau, Papua New Guinea, the Philippines (Philippine English), Puerto Rico, Rwanda, the Solomon Islands, Saint Lucia, Samoa, Seychelles, Sierra Leone, Sri Lanka, Swaziland, Tanzania, Uganda, Zambia, and Zimbabwe. It is also one of the 11 official languages that are given equal status in South Africa (South African English). English is also the official language in current dependent territories of Australia (Norfolk Island, Christmas Island and Cocos Island) and of the United States (Northern Mariana Islands, American Samoa and Puerto Rico), former British colony of Hong Kong, and Netherlands Antilles.

English is an important language in several former colonies and protectorates of the United Kingdom but falls short of official status, such as in Malaysia, Brunei, United Arab Emirates and Bahrain. English is also not an official language in either the United States or the United Kingdom. Although the United States federal government has no official languages, English has been given official status by 30 of the 50 state governments. English is not a de jure official language of Israel; however, the country has maintained official language use a de facto role for English since the British mandate.

Because English is so widely spoken, it has often been referred to as a "world language", the lingua franca of the modern era While English is not an official language in most countries, it is currently the language most often taught as a second language around the world. Some linguists believe that it is no longer the exclusive cultural sign of "native English speakers", but is rather a language that is absorbing aspects of cultures worldwide as it continues to grow. It is, by international treaty, the official language for aerial and maritime communications. English is an official language of the United Nations and many other international organisations, including the International Olympic Committee.

English is the language most often studied as a foreign language in the European Union, followed by French, German, and Spanish. In the EU, a large fraction of the population reports being able to converse to some extent in English. Among non-English speaking countries, a large percentage of the population claimed to be able to converse in English in the Netherlands, Sweden, Denmark, Luxembourg, Finland, Slovenia, Austria, Belgium, and Germany. Norway and Iceland also have a large majority of competent English-speakers.

1.4. Role of Missionaries

Teaching English as a tool for communicating the story of Jesus has a long history. Missionaries have vehemently differed from one another about its usefulness as a tool for this purpose. Even as English contains excellent Christian literature, it also is home for secular literature. Secular Humanism found its way in many lands through the learning of English language and literature. Its "ennobling" characteristic as a tool and purveyor of culture, the scientific knowledge it opens up for those who learn it, the ease with which one could transact business using it, all have more or less overshadowed the deep Christian foundation upon which the language, literature and culture is built.

Aided by the influence of secularism, many Christian teachers of English have more or less abandoned the Christian programme while teaching English. Ethics and morals portrayed in literature were interpreted not as emerging from the Christian base but from universal humanism. English is still pregnant with Christian metaphors, idioms and set phrases, which cannot be wholly understood and used without a grasp of the underlying Christian message.

The original pieces of writing by the native speakers of English are sought to be replaced by the writings of the nationals who are masters of English prose and poetry. In their creative writing, metaphors, idioms, and set phrases from the national languages, which imply local culture and religion, are more freely used. Translations from the local tales are more frequently substituted for tales from Europe. In addition, government-inspired documents on ideology become part of the textbook. Nations (and individuals) want to appropriate English as a language minus the culture and religion it represents and communicates.

Even as the goals of English teaching and learning are being continually redefined, you should remember that English would not be taught solely by the native speakers of English in many nations. Some countries like India, Pakistan, Nepal, Bangladesh and several African nations have provided for the teaching of English mainly through their nationals. Some countries like Japan and China open their doors to more number of native speakers of English to teach English.

When English is introduced in the school curriculum as a language to be learned in addition to a national language or languages, it is inevitable that governments and institutions would look for training their own nationals to meet the demand. Missionaries in the past responded to this by training nationals in the art of teaching English as a foreign or second language, while noting all the time the inadequate skills attained in pronunciation and naturalness of usage. The missionaries and others involved in teaching English have recognised that a perfect duplication of the native speakers' language is neither possible nor desirable.

1.5. As Global Linqua Franca

Modern English, sometimes described as the first global lingua franca, is the dominant international language in communications, science, business, aviation, entertainment, radio and diplomacy. The initial reason for its enormous spread beyond the bounds of the British Isles, where it was originally a native tongue, was the British Empire, and by the late nineteenth century its reach was truly global. It is the dominant language in the United States, whose growing economic and cultural influence and status as a global superpower since World War II have significantly accelerated adoption of English as a language across the planet.

A working knowledge of English has become a requirement in a number of fields, occupations and professions such as medicine and as a consequence over a billion people speak English to at least a basic level.

Linguists such as David Crystal recognise that one impact of this massive growth of English, in common with other global languages, has been to reduce native linguistic diversity in many parts of the world historically, most particularly in Australasia and North America, and its huge influence continues to play an important role in language attrition. By a similar token, historical linguists, aware of the complex and fluid dynamics of language change, are always alive to the potential English contains through the vast size and spread of the communities that use it and its natural internal variety, such as in its creoles and pidgins, to produce a new family of distinct languages over time.

1.6. As an International Language

English is an international language, spoken in many countries both as a native and as a second or foreign language. It is taught in the schools in almost every country on this earth. It is a living and vibrant language spoken by over 300 million people as their native language. Millions more speak it as an additional language.

English is spoken habitually in the United States, the British Isles, Ireland, Canada, Australia, New Zealand, the Republic of South Africa, Liberia, and many territories under the United

Kingdom and the United States of America. It is estimated that 300 million people speak English as a second language, and an additional 100 million people use it fluently as a foreign language. As a rough estimate, 1000 million or one billion people around the world have some knowledge of English, either as a native language, as a second language, or as a foreign language.

English is the associate official language of India which has over 1000 million (over billion) people. Pakistan, Bangladesh, and many other nations which were ruled by Britain continue to use English both as an optional medium of instruction in their schools and as one of their official languages. The islands of the Philippines continue to use English as an important tool for education, administration, and for mass media purposes. English is the chief foreign language taught in the schools of Europe, South America, Asia and Africa.

Even though some nations which were ruled by the French continue to teach French as their most preferred second language, English is gaining ground even in these countries. In the former Soviet Union, Russian was the dominant language. Since the break of the Soviet Union, the Central Asian Republics have been rapidly introducing English in their school system as a second or foreign language. In Russia itself, English is gaining ground as the most popular second language. In Japan too, English is the most favored second or foreign language.

Outside Europe, English is the predominant language of international commerce. Although the United Nations and its various agencies have more than one language for transaction, more often than not, English comes to be chosen as the preferred language of communication between the participating member-nations. All this has happened within the last one hundred years. The ascendancy of English as the most preferred language began two hundred years ago with the colonisation of North America, Asia, and Africa by Britain. The Industrial Revolution in Britain, its ever-expanding maritime power, development of material wealth, progress in scientific research and consequent power, all helped the spread of English, even as Britain marched as a great empire. In the Sixteenth Century, English was spoken mostly in England, southern Scotland, and small areas of Wales and Ireland. There were only about two to three million people speaking it as their native language. At present one in seven in this world speak English either as a native language or as a second language.

Latin was the main medium of education in western Europe throughout the Middle Ages. French was the language of diplomacy for four centuries, from the 17th to 20th. And yet, at present there is not a single language which can be compared to the position occupied by English as the international language. This is so, even though more people in the world speak Chinese than English as their native language. Spanish may claim a large number of native speakers, but neither Spanish, nor French, nor Russian, nor Chinese can even come close to the level and variety of uses to which English is put in the world.

English is learned everywhere because people have found out that knowledge of English is a passport for better career, better pay, advanced knowledge, and for communication with the entire world. English is also learned for the literature it possesses, and for the variety and rich experience it provides. English has replaced French as the language of diplomacy. In this computer age, English is bound to expand its domains of use everywhere. Everyone wants to appropriate English as their own.

In the Indian subcontinent, English became the dominant language of communication among the educated classes after the famous Minute of Lord Macaulay in 1833.

1.7. As a Global Language

English has now inarguably achieved global status. Whenever we turn on the news to find out what's happening in East Asia, or the Balkans, or Africa, or South America, or practically anywhere, local people are being interviewed and telling us about it in English. To illustrate the point when Pope John Paul II arrived in the Middle East recently to retrace Christ's footsteps and addressed Christians, Muslims and Jews, the pontiff spoke not Latin, not Arabic, not Italian, not Hebrew, not his native Polish. He spoke in English.

Indeed, if one looks at some of the facts about the amazing reach of the English language many would be surprised. English is used in over 90 countries as an official or semi-official language. English is the working language of the Asian trade group ASEAN. It is the de facto working language of 98 per cent of international research physicists and research chemists. It is the official language of the European Central Bank, even though the bank is in Frankfurt and neither Britain nor any other predominantly English-speaking country is a member of the European Monetary Union. It is the language in which Indian parents and black parents in South Africa overwhelmingly wish their children to be educated. It is believed that over one billion people worldwide are currently learning English.

One of the more remarkable aspects of the spread of English around the world has been the extent to which Europeans are adopting it as their internal lingua franca. English is spreading from northern Europe to the south and is now firmly entrenched as a second language in countries such as Sweden, Norway, Netherlands and Denmark. Although not an official language in any of these countries if one visits any of them it would seem that almost everyone there can communicate with ease in English. Indeed, if one switches on a television in Holland one would find as many channels in English (albeit subtitled), as there are in Dutch.

English has without a doubt become the global language.

References

Baugh, Albert C., Thomas Cable, *A history of the English language,* 5th ed., Routledge, 2002.

Bragg, Melvyn, *The Adventure of English: The Biography of a Language,* Arcade Publishing, 2004.

Crystal, David, *English as a Global Language,* Cambridge: Cambridge University Press, 1997.

________________, *The Stories of English,* Allen Lane, 2004.

________________, *The Cambridge encyclopedia of the English language,* 2nd ed., Cambridge University Press, 2003.

Halliday, MAK, *An introduction to functional grammar,* 2nd ed., London: Edward Arnold, 1994.

Hayford, Harrison; Howard P. Vincent, *Reader and Writer,* Houghton Mifflin Company, 1954.

McArthur, T. (ed.), *The Oxford Companion to the English Language,* Oxford University Press, 1992.

Robinson, Orrin, *Old English and Its Closest Relatives,* Stanford Univ. Press, 1992.

2

Approaches to English Language Instruction

2.1. Teaching English Language

Many schools lack the funds to provide effective English language training. Native or fluent English speakers with or without formal teaching experience can contribute greatly to a child's educational development. Good teaching happens when competent teachers with non-discouraging personalities use non-defensive approaches to language teaching and learning, and cherish their students.

Children learn English as a second or foreign language much faster than the adults. They imitate the teacher's pronunciation, sentences, phrases, and words more easily. They do not ask for explicit rules which explain how sentences are put together, produced, and pronounced. They may ask for the meanings of words, but they are able to intuitively identify salient features of the meanings of a word and use the word more or less correctly.

The teacher should be pleasant and sweet-natured, able to communicate at the level of the children. Use of audio-visuals is more important than the printed text. The printed text should be colourful, full of pictures, and should have only few language elements such as words, phrases, and sentences. Language learning should be encouraged in all the classes and in all the environments. Children have a natural curiosity to investigate the environment in greater detail. When they go to the bazaar, the see a lot of signboards and they start reading the same. They start reading the road signs with great interest. The teacher can create a bazaar inside the classroom for reading and conversation purposes. Pretend situations are greatly enjoyed by children, and they do actively participate in such games.

2.2. Activity-based Approach

Children are interested in group activities. Devise group work which would require use of words and sentences for communication among members of the group. Devise group work which aim at accomplishing some language-related task such as language games.

If the textbook lessons are not activity-based, you should be able to convert the lessons in such a way that there are abundant activities built into the teaching of the lesson. Conventional textbooks provide for some activities as part of the exercises. An activity-based lesson centers around the activity to teach the language. Children are given some words and some simple sentences. They are asked to perform a task as a group, conversing with each other. They will use the words and sentences, some in full and most of the time in abbreviated form to communicate with one another. They may use many gestures while performing the task. Ultimately they would achieve what they set out to achieve. They would complete the task and would be greatly involved in doing the task.

Physical activities help in learning the words and sentences. An activity-based approach is always better than mere classroom teaching mode with repetition, imitation drills, etc.

2.2.1. Fluency and Correct Pronunciation

If the fundamentals of motivation, fluency and correct pronunciation are built in a steady manner without overemphasizing correctness of speech at the entry level, and if the teachers themselves have a good command of English with model setting pronunciation capabilities, children will learn English better and faster.

2.2.2. Class Activities

Nursery rhymes and songs acted out help children to internalise some words and sentences. Use nursery rhymes and songs for testing their knowledge and command of English. Use English all the time in the class. However, do not refuse to give brief explanations in the native language of children. But such explanations should have the focus on strengthening the use of

English, not the mastery of translation from one language into another. Do not use the native language to elicit English responses. Use objects and actions instead.

Comics appropriate to children may be used. Children will see the pictures, listen to your reading, and will reproduce in their own language the utterances of the characters in the book as much as they can. Let the children act out the story. This will develop their listening and speaking skills. Reading and writing will take deliberate effort on the part of the students. Reading and writing should be less in quantum than speaking and listening in English classes for children.

Class activities should center around and cover all language skills. However, the extent to which the reading and writing will be covered in a children's class will depend upon the proficiency so far attained. Children, like adults, have some difficulty in mastering the reading and writing skills. Do not accelerate the pace of learning in these skills.

2.3. Models of Language Teaching and Learning

Language instructors are often in one of three situations:

- They are language instructors with experience teaching in their countries of origin
- They are professionals in other fields who are native speakers of the language, but are not trained as teachers
- They are graduate students who have extensive knowledge of language, literature, and culture, but are not trained as language teachers

These instructors often must begin their work in the classroom with little or no guidance to help them appreciate which methods work, how, and why. In response, they may fall back on an outdated model for understanding language teaching and language learning.

2.3.1. Older Model

Language learning is a product of transmission. Teacher transmits knowledge. Learner is recipient. This teacher-centered model views the teacher as active and the student as fundamentally passive. The teacher is responsible for transmitting all of the information to the students. The teacher talks; the students listen and absorb (or take a nap). The teacher-centered model may be attractive to new language instructors for several reasons:

- It is the method by which they were taught
- It makes sense: The teacher should be the focus of the classroom, since the teacher knows the language and the students do not
- It requires relatively little preparation: All the teacher needs to do is present the material outlined in the appropriate chapter of the book
- It requires relatively little thought about student or student activities: All student listen to the same (teacher) presentation, then do related exercises

However, experienced language instructors who reflect on their teaching practice have observed that the teacher-centered model has two major drawbacks:

- It involves only a minority of students in actual language learning
- It gives students knowledge about the language, but does not necessarily enable them to use it for purposes that interest them

To overcome these drawbacks, language teaching professionals in the United States and elsewhere have adopted a different model of teaching and learning.

2.3.2. Newer Model

Language learning is a process of discovery. Learner develops ability to use the language for specific communication purposes. Teacher models language use and facilitates students' development of language skills. In this learner-centered model, both student and teacher are active participants who share responsibility for the student's learning. Instructor and students work together to identify how students expect to use the language. The instructor models correct and appropriate language use, and students then use the language themselves in practice activities that simulate real communication situations. The active, joint engagement of students and teacher leads to a dynamic classroom environment in which teaching and learning become rewarding and enjoyable.

Language instructors who have never experienced learner-centered instruction can find it daunting in several ways.

- *It requires more preparation time:* Instructors must consider students' language learning goals, identify classroom activities that will connect those with the material presented in the textbook, and find appropriate real-world materials to accompany them
- *It is mysterious:* It's not clear what, exactly, an instructor does to make a classroom learner centered
- *It feels like it isn't going to work:* When students first are invited to participate actively, they may be slow to get started as they assess the tasks and figure out classroom dynamics
- *It feels chaotic:* Once student start working in small groups, the classroom becomes noisy and the instructor must be comfortable with the idea that students may make mistakes that are not heard and corrected
- *It sounds like a bad idea:* The phrase "learner centered" makes it sound as though the instructor is not in control of the classroom

In fact, in an effective learner-centered classroom, the instructor has planned the content of all activities, has set time limits on them, and has set them in the context of instructor-modelled language use. The instructor is not always the center of attention, but is still in control of students' learning activities.

2.4. Reflective Teaching Practice

Reflective practice allows instructors to consider these questions in a disciplined way. Reflective practice asks:

- Which teaching model am I using?
- How does it apply in specific teaching situations?
- How well is it working?

Every instructor starts with an initial theory of language teaching and learning, based on personal experiences as a language learner and, in some cases, reading or training. In reflective practice, the teacher applies this theory in classroom practice, observes and reflects on the results, and adapts the theory. The classroom becomes a kind of laboratory where the teacher can relate teaching theory to teaching practice.

The theory provides a unifying rationale for the activities that the instructor uses in the classroom; classroom observation and reflection enable the instructor to refine the theory and adjust teaching practice. Concepts that the teacher acquires through reading and professional development are absorbed into the theory and tested in the reflective practice cycle. This cycle of theory building, practice and reflection continues throughout a teacher's career, as the teacher evaluates new experiences and tests new or adapted theories against them.

2.5. Teaching Portfolios

Reflective practice is aided by the use of a professional portfolio. A teaching portfolio is a record of a teacher's classroom performance, development as a teacher, and building of coherence through reflective practice. The following are the functions of a teaching portfolio:

- To allow a teacher to track personal developmen
- To document teaching practice for performance review
- To illustrate teaching approach for potential employers

2.5.1. Contents of a Teaching Portfolio

2.5.1.1. *Background and philosophy*

- *professional biography*: a narrative description of your professional history and the major influences on your teaching
- *teaching philosophy*: a description of how you teach and why, the theoretical and philosophical foundations of your approach
- information about the environment(s) where you have worked and any relevant details about courses you have taught

2.5.1.2. *Documentation of performance*

- classroom materials and assignments
- syllabi
- assessments
- professional development activities
- teaching-oriented professional service

2.5.1.3. *Evaluations*

- student evaluations
- supervisor reports
- letters of support about your teaching

A teaching portfolio can be a valuable tool for you as a language instructor. The reflective work that goes into producing it will encourage you to clarify for yourself what you are doing and why. It will also help you understand the professional value of teaching. Your teaching portfolio will allow you to present both your language teaching philosophy and the best or most interesting examples of its application in the classroom. Your portfolio should not be a static collection that you develop once and never revise; you should review and update it every year so that it reflects your growth as a language teaching professional.

2.5.2. Well Preparation

Effective teaching depends on preparation. Here are eight things to do at the beginning of the semester to help yourself have a rewarding and enjoyable teaching experience.

1. *Content:* Find out what the department expects you to teach and what materials you are expected to use. Review the curriculum or textbook to get a roadmap of the semester as a whole. Working through the curriculum should be a process of discovery for the students, but not for the instructor.
2. *Method:* Find out what teaching approach you are expected to use. Are you expected to stick closely to the textbook, or to bring in outside materials to supplement? Is your teaching practice expected to be more learner centered or

more teacher centered? Are you expected to teach grammar overtly, or just explain it as it comes up in various contexts?

3. *Students:* Find out what level your students will be. If they are "second year" or "intermediate," ask what that means. What have they studied previously? What materials have they used? This will let you know what to expect from them.
4. *Plan:* Outline a plan for the semester, even if the department has given you a plan. Know when and how you will introduce new material and when and how you will review. What will you do when you get behind? It always happens.
5. *Orientation:* Find out what facilities are available for students and where they are: language lab, computer lab, library. Make a reference card for yourself with the hours when labs are open. Then, when students ask, you won't look like a doofus.
6. *Relationships:* Learn the names of your students as soon as you can. Use their names when talking with them and when giving language examples in class. Attending to your students as individuals will help you assess their progress more effectively. Also, if students believe that you care about them, they will care about you.
7. *Expectations:* Ask how much and what kind of homework is usually given to students at the level you are teaching. Find out what expectations the department has for frequency and type of testing. Let your students know what the expectations are in these areas.
8. *Guidance:* Ask your supervisor or another experienced instructor to serve as your mentor. A mentor can review your plan for the semester before classes start to be sure you're on the right track, and can meet with you on a regular basis throughout the semester to answer questions and give you support when you need it. Having a mentor is especially important toward the end of the first semester of teaching, when many teachers begin to feel overwhelmed, discouraged, or frustrated.

2.6. Teaching Goals and Methods

2.6.1. Communicative Competence

Communicative competence is made up of four competence areas: linguistic, sociolinguistic, discourse, and strategic.

- Linguistic competence is knowing how to use the grammar, syntax, and vocabulary of a language. Linguistic competence asks: What words do I use? How do I put them into phrases and sentences?
- Sociolinguistic competence is knowing how to use and respond to language appropriately, given the setting, the topic, and the relationships among the people communicating. Sociolinguistic competence asks: Which words and phrases fit this setting and this topic? How can I express a specific attitude (courtesy, authority, friendliness, respect) when I need to? How do I know what attitude another person is expressing?
- Discourse competence is knowing how to interpret the larger context and how to construct longer stretches of language so that the parts make up a coherent whole. Discourse competence asks: How are words, phrases and sentences put together to create conversations, speeches, email messages, newspaper articles?
- Strategic competence is knowing how to recognise and repair communication breakdowns, how to work around gaps in one's knowledge of the language, and how to learn more about the language and in the context. Strategic competence asks: How do I know when I've misunderstood or when someone has misunderstood me? What do I say then? How can I express my ideas if I don't know the name of something or the right verb form to use?

In the early stages of language learning, instructors and students may want to keep in mind the goal of communicative efficiency: That learners should be able to make themselves understood, using their current proficiency to the fullest. They should try to avoid confusion in the message (due to faulty pronunciation, grammar, or vocabulary); to avoid offending communication partners (due to socially inappropriate style); and to use strategies for recognising and managing communication breakdowns.

2.6.2. Learner-centered Instruction

In language classrooms, instruction focuses on the learner and the learning process. The instructor creates a learning environment that resembles as much as possible the one in which students learned their first language. Students participate in the learning process by establishing learning goals, developing and choosing learning strategies, and evaluating their own progress. In the classroom, students attend to models provided by the instructor (input) and then build on those models as they use language themselves (output). Classroom activities incorporate real-world situations.

Learner-centered instruction encourages students to take responsibility for their own language skill development and helps them gain confidence in their ability to learn and use the language. Teachers support students by devoting some class time to non-traditional activities, including teaching learners how to use learning strategies, how to use available tools and resources, and how to reflect on their own learning.

Students who are accustomed to more traditional teacher-centered instruction may resist the learner-centered model at first because it expects them to be more involved in the learning process. However, when they discover that learner-centered instruction enables them to develop real-world language skills while having fun, they usually become enthusiastic participants.

These ten guidelines will help you make communicative language teaching and learner-centered instruction part of your own instructional approach.

- Provide appropriate input
- Use language in authentic ways
- Provide context
- Design activities with a purpose
- Use task-based activities
- Encourage collaboration
- Use an integrated approach
- Address grammar consciously
- Adjust feedback/error correction to the situation
- Include awareness of cultural aspects of language use

2.6.2.1. *Provide Appropriate Input*

Input is the language to which students are exposed: teacher talk, listening activities, reading passages, and the language heard and read outside of class. Input gives learners the material they need to develop their ability to use the language on their own. Language input has two forms.

Finely tuned input

- Is matched to learners' current comprehension level and connected to what they already know
- Focuses on conscious learning of a specific point: the pronunciation of a word, the contrast in the uses of two verb tenses, new vocabulary, useful social formulas
- Is controlled by the instructor or textbook author
- Is used in the presentation stage of a lesson

Roughly tuned input

- Is more complex than learners' current proficiency and stretches the boundaries of their current knowledge
- Focuses on authentic use of language in listening or reading passages
- Is used "as is," with minimal alteration by the instructor or textbook author
- Is used in the activity stage of the lesson

Roughly tuned input challenges student to use listening and reading strategies to aid comprehension. When selecting authentic materials for use as roughly tuned input, look for listening and reading selections that are one level of proficiency higher than students' current level. This will ensure that students will be challenged by the material without being overwhelmed by its difficulty.

2.6.2.2. *Use Language in Authentic Ways*

In order to learn a language, instead of merely learning about it, students need as much as possible to hear and read the language as native speakers use it. Instructors can make this happen in two ways.

Teacher talk: Always try to use the language as naturally as possible when you are talking to students. Slowing down may seem to make the message more comprehensible, but it also distorts the subtle shifts in pronunciation that occur in naturally paced speech.

- Speak at a normal rate
- Use vocabulary and sentence structures with which students are familiar
- State the same idea in different ways to aid comprehension

Materials: Give students authentic reading material from newspapers, magazines, and other print sources. To make them accessible,

- Review them carefully to ensure that the reading level is appropriate
- Introduce relevant vocabulary and grammatical structures in advance
- Provide context by describing the content and typical formats for the type of material (for example, arrival and departure times for travel schedules)

Advertisements, travel brochures, packaging, and street signs contain short statements that students at lower levels can manage. The World Wide Web is a rich resource for authentic materials. Reading authentic materials motivates students at all levels because it gives them the sense that they really are able to use the language.

2.6.2.3. *Provide Context*

Context includes knowledge of

- the topic or content
- the vocabulary and language structures in which the content is usually presented
- the social and cultural expectations associated with the content

To help students have an authentic experience of understanding and using language, prepare them by raising their awareness of the context in which it occurs.

- Ask them what they know about the topic
- Ask what they can predict from the title or heading of a reading selection or the opening line of a listening selection
- Review the vocabulary (including idiomatic expressions) and sentence structures that are usually found in that type of material
- Review relevant social and cultural expectations

2.6.2.4. *Design Activities with a Purpose*

Activities in the language classroom simulate communication outside the classroom when they are structured with such a purpose. In these classroom activities, students use the language to fill an information gap by getting answers or expanding a partial understanding. For example, students work in pairs, and each is given half of a map, grid, or list needed to complete a task. The pair then talk to each other until they both have all the information.

2.6.2.5. *Use Task-based Activities*

Fluent speakers use language to perform tasks such as solving problems, developing plans, and working together to complete projects. The use of similar task-based activities in the classroom is an excellent way to encourage students to use the language. Tasks may involve solving a word problem, creating a crossword puzzle, making a video, preparing a presentation, or drawing up a plan.

2.6.2.6. *Encourage Collaboration*

Whenever possible, ask students to work in pairs or small groups. Give students structure in the form of a defined task and outcome. This structure will allow students to collaborate as they develop a work plan, discuss the substance of the task, and report the outcome. They will thus use language in a variety of ways and learn from each other. Effective collaborative activities have three characteristics.

- *Communication gap:* Each student has relevant information that the others don't have

- *Task orientation:* Activity has a defined outcome, such as solving a problem or drawing a map
- *Time limit:* Students have a preset amount of time to complete the task

2.6.2.7. *Use an Integrated Approach*

Integration has two forms. Mode integration is the combination of listening, speaking, reading, and writing in classroom activities. By asking students to use two or more modes, instructors create activities that imitate real world language use.

Content integration is bringing content from students' fields of study into the language curriculum. University students often find it instructive to read, discuss, and write about material whose content they already know, because their knowledge of the topic helps them understand and use the language. They are able to scaffold: to build on existing knowledge as they increase their language proficiency. For students who plan to study and/or work in a field that will require them to use the language they are learning, integration of content can be a powerful motivator.

2.6.2.8. *Address Grammar Consciously*

University students usually need and appreciate direct instruction in points of grammar that are related to classroom activities. These students often have knowledge of the rules associated with standard use of their native language (metalinguistic knowledge) and can benefit from development of similar knowledge in the target language and discussion of similarities and differences.

Discuss points of grammar in the contexts where they arise. Asking students to think through a rule in the context of an effort to express themselves clearly is a more effective way of helping them internalise the rule than teaching the rule in isolation. Two types of grammar rules to address when using authentic materials:

- *Prescriptive rules:* State how the language "should" or "must" be used; define what is "correct." These are the rules that are taught in language textbooks.
- *Descriptive rules:* State how the language is actually used by fluent speakers. The degree to which descriptive rules

differ from prescriptive rules depends on the setting (casual/formal use of language), the topic, and the backgrounds of the speakers.

2.6.2.9. *Adjust Feedback/Error Correction to Situation*

In the parts of a lesson that focus on form, direct and immediate feedback is needed and expected. Encourage students to self-correct by waiting after they have spoken or by asking them to try again. The following are the feedback techniques:

- Paraphrase a student's utterances, modelling the correct forms .
- Ask students to clarify their utterances, providing paraphrases of their own.

Avoid feeding students the correct forms every time. Gradually teaching them to depend less on you and more on themselves is what language teaching is all about. In the parts of a lesson that focus on communication activities, the flow of talk should not be interrupted by the teacher's corrections. When students address you, react to the content of their utterances, not just the form. Your response is a useful comprehension check for students, and on the affective level it shows that you are listening to what they say.

2.6.2.10. *Include Awareness of Cultural Aspects of Language Use*

Languages are cognitive systems, but they also express ideas and transmit cultural values. When you are discussing language use with your students, it is important to include information on the social, cultural, and historical context that certain language forms carry for native speakers. Often these explanations include reference to what a native speaker would say, and why. Culture is expressed and transmitted through magazines and newspapers, radio and television programs, movies, and the internet. Using media as authentic materials in the classroom can expand students' perspectives and generate interesting discussions about the relationships between language and culture.

2.7. Lesson Planning

A key aspect of effective teaching is having a plan for what will happen in the classroom each day. Creating such a plan involves setting realistic goals, deciding how to incorporate course textbooks and other required materials, and developing activities that will promote learning.

2.7.1. Lesson Goals

Lesson goals are most usefully stated in terms of what students will have done or accomplished at the end of the lesson. Stating goals in this way allows both teacher and learners to know when the goals have been reached. Following are the steps to set lesson goals:

1. Identify a topic for the lesson. The topic is not a goal, but it will help you develop your goals. The topic may be determined largely by your curriculum and textbook. If you have some flexibility in choice of topic, consider your students' interests and the availability of authentic materials at the appropriate level.
2. Identify specific linguistic content, such as vocabulary and points of grammar or language use, to be introduced or reviewed. These are usually prescribed by the course textbook or course curriculum. If they are not, select points that are connected in some significant way with the topic of the lesson.
3. Identify specific communication tasks to be completed by students. To be authentic, the tasks should allow, but not require, students to use the vocabulary, grammar, and strategies presented in the lesson. The focus of the tasks should be topical, not grammatical. This means that it may be possible for some students to complete the task without using either the grammar point or the strategy presented in the first part of the lesson.
4. Identify specific learning strategies to be introduced or reviewed in connection with the lesson.
5. Create goal statements for the linguistic content, communication tasks, and learning strategies that state what you will do and what students will do during the lesson.

2.7.2. Structure the Lesson

A language lesson should include a variety of activities that combine different types of language input and output. Learners at all proficiency levels benefit from such variety; research has shown that it is more motivating and is more likely to result in effective language learning. An effective lesson has five parts:

- Preparation
- Presentation
- Practice
- Evaluation
- Expansion

The five parts of a lesson may all take place in one class session or may extend over multiple sessions, depending on the nature of the topic and the activities.

The lesson plan should outline who will do what in each part of the lesson. The time allotted for preparation, presentation, and evaluation activities should be no more than 8-10 minutes each. Communication practice activities may run a little longer.

2.7.2.1. Preparation

As the class begins, give students a broad outline of the day's goals and activities so they know what to expect. Help them focus by eliciting their existing knowledge of the day's topics.

- Use discussion or homework review to elicit knowledge related to the grammar and language use points to be covered
- Use comparison with the native language to elicit strategies that students may already be using
- Use discussion of what students do and/or like to do to elicit their knowledge of the topic they will address in communication activities

2.7.2.2. Presentation

Presentation provides the language input that gives students the foundation for their knowledge of the language. Input comes from the instructor and from course textbooks. Language textbooks designed for students in U.S. universities usually provide input only in the form of examples; explanations and instructions are written in English. To increase the amount of input that students receive in the target language, instructors should use it as much as possible for all classroom communication purposes.

An important part of the presentation is structured output, in which students practice the form that the instructor has presented. In structured output, accuracy of performance is important. Structured output is designed to make learners comfortable producing specific language items recently introduced. Structured output is a type of communication that is found only in language classrooms. Because production is limited to pre-selected items, structured output is not truly communicative.

2.7.2.3. *Practice*

In this part of the lesson, the focus shifts from the instructor as presenter to the students as completers of a designated task. Students work in pairs or small groups on a topic-based task with a specific outcome. Completion of the task may require the bridging of an information gap. The instructor observes the groups an acts as a resource when students have questions that they cannot resolve themselves.

In their work together, students move from structured output to communicative output, in which the main purpose is to complete the communication task. Language becomes a tool, rather than an end in itself. Learners have to use any or all of the language that they know along with varied communication strategies. The criterion of success is whether the learner gets the message across. Accuracy is not a consideration unless the lack of it interferes with the message.

Activities for the practice segment of the lesson may come from a textbook or be designed by the instructor.

2.7.2.4. *Evaluation*

When all students have completed the communication practice task, reconvene the class as a group to recap the lesson. Ask students to give examples of how they used the linguistic content and learning or communication strategies to carry out the communication task. Evaluation is useful for four reasons:

- It reinforces the material that was presented earlier in the lesson
- It provides an opportunity for students to raise questions of usage and style
- It enables the instructor to monitor individual student comprehension and learning
- It provides closure to the lesson

2.7.2.5. *Expansion*

Expansion activities allow students to apply the knowledge they have gained in the classroom to situations outside it. Expansion activities include out-of-class observation assignments, in which the instructor asks students to find examples of something or to use a strategy and then report back.

2.7.3. Materials and Activities

The materials for a specific lesson will fall into two categories: those that are required, such as course textbooks and lab materials, and authentic materials that the teacher incorporates into classroom activities. For required materials, determine what information must be presented in class and decide which exercise(s) to use in class and which for out-of-class work. For teacher-provided materials, use materials that are genuinely related to realistic communication activities. Truly authentic communication tasks have several features:

- They involve solving a true problem or discussing a topic of interest
- They require using language to accomplish a goal, not using language merely to use language
- They allow students to use all of the language skills they have, rather than specific forms or vocabulary, and to self-correct when they realise they need to
- The criterion of success is clear: completion of a defined task

2.8. Language Acquisition

To become engaged learners, students need to understand that learning a language is not the same as learning *about* a language. When students think of the language as a school subject like any other, they may learn a great deal about its vocabulary, grammar, and sentence and discourse structure, but the language will not become a true medium of communication for them and won't engage them very deeply. Students need to understand that learning a language means becoming able to use it to comprehend, communicate, and think – as they do in their first language.

Students also need to recognise that language learning takes place in stages. Interpretive skills (listening, reading) develop much more quickly than expressive skills (speaking, writing), and the ability that students covet most—the ability to speak the second language fluently—requires the longest period of growth. All language learners have to work through a sequence of "approximate" versions called interlanguages (ILs), each of which represents a level of understanding of the target language.

The following features of ILs can help teachers and learners understand and monitor the language learning process.

- *Uniqueness:* ILs vary significantly from learner to learner in the early stages of language learning. Learners impose rules of their own on the oral and written input they receive. Each learner does this differently, combining emerging understanding of the rules of the new language with ideas derived from the first language and other information that comes from their individual situations and backgrounds.
- *Systematicity:* As learners begin to develop proficiency in a language, they make errors in systematic ways. For example, once students learn the inflections for a single class of verbs, they may apply them to all classes indiscriminately. These errors are based on systematic assumptions, or false rules, about the language. When students become aware of this aspect of their language skill development, they often appreciate and even ask for overt error correction from the instructor.
- *Fossilisation:* Some false rules become more firmly imprinted on the IL than others and are harder for learners to overcome. Fossilisation results when these false rules become permanent features of a learner's use of the language.

- *Convergence:* As learners' rules come to approximate more closely those of the language they are learning, convergence sets in. This means that learners who come from different native language backgrounds make similar assumptions and formulate similar hypotheses about the rules of the new language, and therefore make similar errors.

Instructors can help students understand the process of language skill development in several ways.

(a) Focus on interlanguage as a natural part of language learning; remind them that they learned their first language this way.

(b) Point out that the systematic nature of interlanguage can help students understand why they make errors. They can often predict when they will make errors and what types of errors they will make.

(c) Keep the overall focus of the classroom on communication, not error correction. Use overt correction only in structured output activities.

(d) Teach students that mistakes are learning opportunities. When their errors interfere with their ability to communicate, they must develop strategies for handling the misunderstanding that results.

2.9. Engagement in Language Learning

When the successful language learner is one who can pass tests and make good grades, learning about the language is all that is required and success is defined by mastery of rules and forms. When the successful language learner is one who has the ability to use the language to accomplish communication goals, success is defined as making the language one's own. To promote engagement in language learning:

- Encourage students to use the language spontaneously to communicate ideas, feelings, and opinions
- Identify informal out-of-class language learning experiences
- Ask students to evaluate their progress in terms of increases in their functional proficiency

Students' motivation for learning a language increases when they see connections between what they do in the classroom and what they hope to do with the language in the future. Their attention increases when classroom activities are relevant to their other interests. To make these connections, begin by having students list the ways they may use the language in future. Have them include both the ways they plan to use it and other ways that might arise. Ask them to be as specific as possible. For each way of using language, ask them to list specific communication tasks that they will need to be able to do. Use these purposes and tasks as the basis for task-oriented classroom communication activities.

Some lower level students will respond that they don't plan to use the language – that they are taking the course to fulfill a university language requirement. Encourage these students to develop an imaginary scenario for themselves in which they have some reason for using the language. In doing this, some students may think of ways in which they really might use it, and others will come to understand that purpose is an integral part of language learning.

2.10. Learning Strategies Instruction

Students learning a language have two kinds of knowledge working for them:

- Their knowledge of their first language
- Their awareness of learning strategies, the mechanisms they use, consciously or unconsciously, to manage the absorption of new material

Students differ as language learners in part because of differences in ability, motivation, or effort, but a major difference lies in their knowledge about and skill in using "how to learn" techniques, that is, learning strategies. Classroom research demonstrates the role of learning strategies in effective language learning:

- Good learners are able to identify the best strategy for a specific task; poor learners have difficulty choosing the best strategy for a specific task
- Good learners are flexible in their approach and adopt a different strategy if the first one doesn't work; poor

learners have a limited variety of strategies in their repertoires and stay with the first strategy they have chosen even when it doesn't work

- Good learners have confidence in their learning ability; poor learners lack confidence in their learning ability
- Good learners expect to succeed, fulfill their expectation, and become more motivated; poor learners: expect to do poorly, fulfill their expectation, and lose motivation

Learning strategies instruction shows students that their success or lack of it in the language classroom is due to the way they go about learning rather than to forces beyond their control. Most students can learn how to use strategies more effectively; when they do so, they become more self reliant and better able to learn independently. They begin to take more responsibility for their own learning, and their motivation increases because they have increased confidence in their learning ability and specific techniques for successful language learning.

Instructors can tap into students' knowledge about how languages work and how learning happens – their metacognition—to help them direct and monitor the language learning process in two ways:

- By encouraging them to recognise their own thinking processes, developing self-knowledge that leads to self-regulation: planning how to proceed with a learning task, monitoring one's own performance on an ongoing basis, and evaluating learning and self as learner upon task completion. Students with greater metacognitive awareness understand the similarity between the current learning task and previous ones, know the strategies required for successful learning, and anticipate success as a result of knowing how to learn.
- By describing specific learning strategies, demonstrating their application to designated learning tasks, and having students practice using them. In order to continue to be successful with learning tasks, students need to be aware of the strategies that led to their success and recognise the value of using them again. By devoting class time to learning strategies, teachers reiterate their importance and value.

To teach language learning strategies effectively, instructors should do several things:

- Build on strategies students already use by finding out their current strategies and making students aware of the range of strategies used by their classmates
- Integrate strategy instruction with regular lessons, rather than teaching the strategies separately from language learning activities
- Be explicit: name the strategy, tell students why and how it will help them, and demonstrate its use
- Provide choice by letting students decide which strategies work best for them
- Guide students in transferring a familiar strategy to new problems
- Plan continuous instruction in language learning strategies throughout the course
- Use the target language as much as possible for strategies instruction.

References

Harmer, J., *The practice of English language teaching*, London: Longman, 1991.

Kramsch, C., *Context and culture in language teaching*, New York: Oxford University Press, 1993.

Lightbown, P., & Spada, N., *How languages are learned*, Oxford: Oxford University Press, 1992.

Oxford, R., & Cohen, A., "Language learning strategies: Critical issues of concept and classification", *Applied Language Learning*, 1992.

Schön, D., *The reflective practitioner: How professionals think in action*, New York: Basic Books, 1983.

Seldin, P., *The teaching portfolio: A practical guide to improved performance and promotion/tenure decisions*, Bolton, MA: Anker Publishing, 1991.

Wallace, M. J., *Training foreign language teachers: A reflective approach*, New York: Cambridge University Press, 1991.

3

Methods of Teaching English

Innovation in foreign language teaching began in the 19th century and, very rapidly, in the 20th century, leading to a number of different methodologies, sometimes conflicting, each trying to be a major improvement over the last or other contemporary methods. The earliest applied linguists, such as Henry Sweet, Otto Jespersen and Harold Palmer worked on setting principles and approaches based on linguistic and psychological theories, although they left many of the specific practical details for others to devise.

Older methods and approaches such as the grammar translation method or the direct method are disposed of and even ridiculed as newer methods and approaches are invented and promoted as the only and complete solution to the problem of the high failure rates of foreign language students. Most books on language teaching list the various methods that have been used in the past, often ending with the author's new method. These new methods seem to be created full-blown from the authors' minds, as they generally give no credence to what was done before and how it relates to the new method. For example, descriptive linguists seem to claim unhesitatingly that before their work, which lead to the audio-lingual method developed for the U.S. Army in World War II, there were no scientifically-based language teaching methods. However, there is significant evidence to the contrary. It is also often inferred or even stated that older methods were completely ineffective or have died out completely when even the oldest methods are still used. Much of the reason for this is that proponents of new methods have been so sure that their ideas are so new and so correct that they could not conceive that the older ones have enough validity to cause controversy and emphasis on new scientific advances has tended to blind researchers to precedents in older work.

Language education usually takes place at a language school. There are many methods of teaching languages. Some have fallen into relative obscurity and others are widely used; still others have a small following, but offer useful insights. While sometimes confused, the terms "approach", "method" and "technique" are hierarchical concepts. An approach is a set of correlative assumptions about the nature of language and language learning, but does not involve procedure or provide any details about how such assumptions should translate into the classroom setting. Such can be related to second language acquisition theory.

There are three principal views at this level:

The structural view treats language as a system of structurally related elements to code meaning (e.g. grammar). The functional view sees language as a vehicle to express or accomplish a certain function, such as requesting something. The interactive view sees language as a vehicle for the creation and maintenance of social relations, focusing on patters of moves, acts, negotiation and interaction found in conversational exchanges. This view has been fairly dominant since the 1980s.

A method is a plan for presenting the language material to be learned and should be based upon a selected approach. In order for an approach to be translated into a method, an instructional system must be designed considering the objectives of the teaching/learning, how the content is to be selected and organized, the types of tasks to be performed, the roles of students and the roles of teachers. A technique is a very specific, concrete strategem or trick designed to accomplish an immediate objective. Such are derived from the controlling method, and less-directly, with the approach.

3.1. Principles of Language Learning

Language learning principles are generally sorted into three sub-groupings: *Cognitive Principles, Affective Principals* and *Linguistic Principles*. Principles are seen as theory derived from research, to which teachers need to match classroom practices.

3.1.1. Cognitive Principles

- *Automaticity:* Subconscious processing of language with peripheral attention to language forms;
- *Meaningful Learning:* This can be contrasted to *Rote Learning,* and is thought to lead to better long term retention;
- *Anticipation of Rewards:* Learners are driven to act by the anticipation of rewards, tangible or intangible;
- *Intrinsic Motivation:* The most potent learning "rewards" are intrinsically motivated within the learner;
- *Strategic Investment:* The time and learning strategies learners invest into the language learning process.

3.1.2. Affective Principles

- *Language Ego:* Learning a new language involves developing a new mode of thinking—a new language "ego";
- Self-Confidence: Success in learning something can be equated to the belief in learners that they *can* learn it;
- Risk-Taking: Taking risks and experimenting "beyond" what is certain creates better long-term retention;
- Language-Culture Connection: Learning a language also involves learning about cultural values and thinking.

3.1.3. Linguistic Principles

- *Native Language Effect:* A learner's native language creates both facilitating and interfering effects on learning;
- *Interlanguage:* At least some of the learner's development in a new language can be seen as systematic;
- *Communicative Competence:* Fluency and *use* are just as important as accuracy and *usage*—instruction needs to be aimed at organisational, pragmatic and strategic competence as well as psychomotor skills.

Europe and Asia have had a long tradition of teaching and learning foreign languages. Memorisation of vocabulary and translation of sentences often formed the major part of such learning processes in the past. Ancient languages such as Sanskrit and Pali were mastered in Asia through the process of memorisation of texts and vocabulary lists. Learning vocabulary lists indeed formed the core of language learning.

The progress of Reformation in Europe brought within its wake change in methods of learning foreign and classical languages. While writing paradigms for individual verbs continued to be emphasized, teachers began to focus more on oral aspects of language. Until then learning a language was synonymous with learning the written language.

3.2. Grammar Translation Method

Latin and Ancient Greek are known as "dead" languages, based on the fact that people no longer speak them for the purpose of interactive communication. Yet they are still acknowledged as important languages to learn (especially Latin) for the purpose of gaining access to classical literature, and up until fairly recently, for the kinds of grammar training that led to the mental dexterity considered so important in any higher education study stream.

Latin has been studied for centuries, with the prime objectives of learning how to read classical Latin texts, understanding the fundamentals of grammar and translation, and gaining insights into some important foreign influences Latin has had on the development of other European languages. The method used to teach it overwhelmingly bore those objectives in mind, and came to be known as the *Classical Method.* It is now more commonly known in Foreign Language Teaching circles as the *Grammar Translation Method.*

It is hard to decide which is more surprising—the fact that this method has survived right up until today (alongside a host of more modern and more "enlightened" methods), or the fact that what was essentially a method developed for the study of "dead" languages involving little or no spoken communication or listening comprehension is still used for the study of languages that are very much alive and require competence not only in terms of reading, writing and structure, but also speaking, listening and interactive communication.

Most teachers who employ the Grammar Translation Method to teach English would probably tell you that (for their students at least) the most fundamental reason for learning the language is give learners access to English literature, develop their minds "mentally" through foreign language learning, and to build in them the kinds of grammar, reading, vocabulary and translation skills necessary to pass any one of a variety of mandatory written tests required at High School or Tertiary level.

Some teachers who use the method might also tell you that it is the most effective way to prepare students for "global communication" by beginning with the key skills of reading and grammar. Such teachers are probably even unware that the method has a name and can be compared alongside other methods.

3.2.1. Features

The following are the key features of the Grammar Translation Method:

1) Classes are taught in the mother tongue, with little active use of the target language.
2) Much vocabulary is taught in the form of lists of isolated words.
3) Long elaborate explanations of the intricacies of grammar are given.
4) Grammar provides the rules for putting words together, and instruction often focuses on the form and inflection of words.
5) Reading of difficult classical texts is begun early.
6) Little attention is paid to the content of texts, which are treated as exercises in grammatical analysis.
7) Often the only drills are exercises in translating disconnected sentences from the target language into the mother tongue.
8) Little or no attention is given to pronunciation.

3.2.2. Techniques

Diane Larsen-Freeman, in her book *Techniques and Principles in Language Teaching* provides expanded descriptions of some common/typical techniques closely associated with the Grammar Translation Method. Some of these are follows:

1) Translation of a Literary Passage
(Translating target language to native language)
2) Reading Comprehension Questions
(Finding information in a passage, making inferences and relating to personal experience)
3) Antonyms/Synonyms
(Finding antonyms and synonyms for words or sets of words).
4) Cognates
(Learning spelling/sound patterns that correspond between L1 and the target language)
5) Deductive Application of Rule
(Understanding grammar rules and their exceptions, then applying them to new examples)
6) Fill-in-the-blanks
(Filling in gaps in sentences with new words or items of a particular grammar type).
7) Memorisation
(Memorising vocabulary lists, grammatical rules and grammatical paradigms)
8) Use Words in Sentences
(Students create sentences to illustrate they know the meaning and use of new words)
9) Composition
(Students write about a topic using the target language)

3.3. Direct Method

Teachers, frustrated by the limits of the Grammar Translation Method in terms of its inability to create communicative competence in students, began to experiment with new ways of teaching language. Basically, teachers began attempting to teach foreign languages in a way that was more similar to first language acquisition. It incorporated techniques designed to address all the areas that the Grammar Translation did not—namely oral communication, more spontaneous use of the language, and developing the ability to think in the target language.

The appearance of the "Direct Method" thus coincided with a new school of thinking that dictated that all foreign language teaching should occur in the target language only, with no translation and an emphasis on linking *meaning* to the language being learned. The method became very popular during the first quarter of the 20th century, especially in private language schools in Europe where highly motivated students could study new languages and not need to travel far in order to try them out and apply them communicatively. One of the most famous advocates of the Direct Method was the German Charles Berlitz, whose schools and Berlitz Method are now world-renowned.

Still, the Direct Method was not without its problems. As Brown points out, "(it) did not take well in public education where the constraints of budget, classroom size, time, and teacher background made such a method difficult to use." By the late 1920s, the method was starting to go into decline and there was even a return to the Grammar Translation Method, which guaranteed more in the way of scholastic language learning orientated around reading and grammar skills. But the Direct Method continues to enjoy a popular following in private language school circles, and it was one of the foundations upon which the well-known "Audiolingual Method" expanded from starting half way through the 20th century.

Objectives include teaching the students how to use the language spontaneously and orally, linking meaning with the target language through the use of realia, pictures or pantomime. There is to be a *direct* connection between concepts and the language to be learned.

3.3.1. Features

The following are the key features of the Direct Method:

1) Classroom instruction is conducted exclusively in the target language.
2) Only everyday vocabulary and sentences are taught.
3) Oral communication skills are built up in a carefully traded progression organised around question-and-answer exchanges between teachers and students in small, intensive classes.
4) Grammar is taught inductively.

5) New teaching points are taught through modelling and practice.
6) Concrete vocabulary is taught through demonstration, objects, and pictures; abstract vocabulary is taught by association of ideas.
7) Both speech and listening comprehension are taught.
8) Correct pronunciation and grammar are emphasized.

3.4. Audiolingual Method

The next revolution in terms of language teaching methodology coincided with World War II, when America became aware that it needed people to learn foreign languages very quickly as part of its overall military operations. The "Army Method" was suddenly developed to build communicative competence in translators through very intensive language courses focusing on aural/oral skills. This in combination with some new ideas about language learning coming from the disciplines of descriptive linguistics and behavioural psychology went on to become what is known as the Audiolingual Method (ALM).

Just as with the Direct Method that preceded it, the overall goal of the Audiolingual Method was to create *communicative* competence in learners. However, it was thought that the most effective way to do this was for students to "overlearn" the language being studied through extensive repetition and a variety of elaborate drills. The idea was to project the linguistic patterns of the language (based on the studies of structural linguists) into the minds of the learners in a way that made responses automatic and "habitual". To this end it was held that the language "habits" of the first language would constantly interfere, and the only way to overcome this problem was to facilitate the learning of a new set of "habits" appropriate linguistically to the language being studied.

3.4.1. Features

The following are the key features of the Audiolingual Method:

1) New material is presented in dialogue form.
2) There is dependence on mimicry, memorisation of set phrases, and overlearning.

3) Structures are sequenced by means of contrastive analysis and taught one at a time.
4) Structural patterns are taught using repetitive drills.
5) There is little or no grammatical explanation. Grammar is taught by inductive analogy rather than deductive explanation.
6) Vocabulary is strictly limited and learned in context.
7) There is much use of tapes, language labs, and visual aids.
8) Great importance is attached to pronunciation.
9) Very little use of the mother tongue by teachers is permitted.
10) Successful responses are immediately reinforced.
11) There is great effort to get students to produce error-free utterances.
12) There is a tendency to manipulate language and disregard content.

The following are the common/typical techniques closely associated with the Audiolingual Method:

1) Dialogue Memorisation

   (Students memorise an opening dialogue using mimicry and applied role-playing)

2) Backward Build-up (Expansion Drill)

   (Teacher breaks a line into several parts, students repeat each part starting at the end of the sentence and "expanding" backwards through the sentence, adding each part in sequence)

3) Repetition Drill

   (Students repeat teacher's model as quickly and accurately as possible)

4) Chain Drill

   (Students ask and answer each other one-by-one in a circular chain around the classroom)

5) Single Slot Substitution Drill

   (Teacher states a line from the dialogue, then uses a word or a phrase as a "cue" that students, when repeating the line, must substitute into the sentence in the correct place)

6) Multiple-slot Substitution Drill

   (Same as the Single Slot drill, except that there are multiple cues to be substituted into the line)

7) Transformation Drill

   (Teacher provides a sentence that must be turned into something else, for example a question to be turned into a statement, an active sentence to be turned into a negative statement, etc)

8) Question-and-answer Drill

   (Students should answer or ask questions very quickly)

9) Use of Minimal Pairs

   (Using contrastive analysis, teacher selects a pair of words that sound identical except for a single sound that typically poses difficulty for the learners—students are to pronounce and differentiate the two words)

10) Complete the Dialogue

    (Selected words are erased from a line in the dialogue—students must find and insert)

11) Grammar Games

    (Various games designed to practice a grammar point in context, using lots of repetition)

3.5. Community Language Learning

In the early seventies, Charles Curran developed a new education model he called "Councelling-Learning". This was essentially an example of an innovative model that primarily considered affective factors as paramount in the learning process. Drawing on Carl Rogers' view that learners were to be considered not as a *class*, but as a *group*, Curran's philosophy dictated that students were to be thought of as "clients"—their needs being addressed by a "councellor" in the form of the teacher. Curran believed that the Councelling-learning model would help lower the instinctive defences adult learners throw up, that the anxiety caused by the educational context could be decreased through the support of an interactive community of fellow learners. Another important goal was for the teacher to be perceived as an empathetic helping agent in the learning process, not a threat.

Community Language Learning seeks to encourage teachers to see their students as "whole" persons, where their feelings, intellect, interpersonal relationships, protective reactions, and desire to learn are addressed and balanced. Students typically sit in a circle, with the teacher (as councellor) outside the ring. They use their first language to develop an interpersonal relationship based on trust with the other students. When a student wants to say something, they first say it in their native language, which the teacher then translates back to them using the target language. The student then attempts to repeat the English used by the teacher, and then a student can respond using the same process. This technique is used over a considerable period of time, until students are able to apply words in the new language without translation, gradually moving from a situation of dependence on the teacher-councellor to a state of independence.

The Community Language Learning method does not just attempt to teach students how to use another language communicatively, it also tries to encourage the students to take increasingly more responsibility for their own learning, and to "learn about their learning", so to speak. Learning in a non-defensive manner is considered to be very important, with teacher and student regarding each other as a "whole person" where intellect and ability are not separated from feelings. The initial struggles with learning the new language are addressed by creating an environment of mutual support, trust and understanding between both learner-clients and the teacher-councellor.

3.5.1. Features

The Community Language Learning method involves some of the following features:

1) Students are to be considered as "learner-clients" and the teacher as a "teacher-councellor".
2) A relationship of mutual trust and support is considered essential to the learning process.
3) Students are permitted to use their native language, and are provided with translations from the teacher which they then attempt to apply.

4) Grammar and vocabulary are taught inductively.
5) "Chunks" of target language produced by the students are recorded and later listened to—they are also transcribed with native language equivalents to become texts the students work with.
6) Students apply the target language independently and without translation when they feel inclined/ confident enough to do so.
7) Students are encouraged to express not only how they feel about the language, but how they feel about the learning process, to which the teacher expresses empathy and understanding.
8) A variety of activities can be included (for example, focusing on a particular grammar or pronunciation point, or creating new sentences based on the recordings/ transcripts).

Some common/typical techniques closely associated with Community Language Learning are as follows:

1) Tape Recording Student Conversation

   (Students choose what they want to say, and their target language production is recorded for later listening/ dissemination)

2) Transcription

   (Teacher produces a transcription of the tape-recorded conversation with translations in the mother language—this is then used for follow up activities or analysis)

3) Reflection on Experience

   (Teacher takes time during or after various activities to allow students to express how they feel about the language and the learning experience, and the teacher indicates empathy/ understanding)

4) Reflective Listening *(Students listen to their own voices on the tape in a relaxed and reflective environment)*

5) Human Computer

   (Teacher is a "human computer" for the students to control—the teacher stating anything in the target language the student wants to practice, giving them the opportunity to self correct)

6) Small Group Tasks

   (Students work in small groups to create new sentences using the transcript, afterwards sharing them with the rest of the class)

3.6. Silent Way

Teachers using the Silent Way want their students to become highly independent and experimental learners. Making errors is a natural part of the process and a key learning device, as it is a sign that students are testing out their hypotheses and arriving at various conclusions about the language through a trial and error style approach. In addition to the idea that students become more autonomous learners and "develop their own inner criteria for correctness", another key objective was to encourage students to work as a group—to try and solve problems in the target language together.

3.6.1. Features

The following are the key theories underlying the Silent Way:

1) Learning is facilitated if the learner discovers or creates rather than remembers and repeats what is to be learned.
2) Learning is facilitated by accompanying (mediating) physical objects.
3) Learning is facilitated by problem-solving involving the material to be learned.

Cuisinere rods (small rods of varying colour and length) are typically used in this method to introduce vocabulary and syntax, along with colourful wall charts. Instruction in this method typically starts with sounds, the basic building blocks in any language. The teacher usually provides single words or short phrases to stimulate the students into refining their knowledge of the language with as little correction/feedback from the teacher as possible.

The following are the some common/typical techniques closely associated with the Silent Way:

1) Sound-Colour Chart

   (The teacher refers students to a colour-coded wall chart depicting individual sounds in the target language—students use this to point out and build words with correct pronunciation)

2) Teacher's Silence

(Teacher is generally silent, only giving help when it is absolutely necessary)

3) Peer Correction

(Students encouraged to help each other in a cooperative and not competitive spirit)

4) Rods

(Rods are used to trigger meaning, and to introduce or actively practice language. They can symbolise whatever words are being taught and be manipulated directly or abstractly to create sentences)

5) Self-correction Gestures

(Teacher uses hands to indicate that something is incorrect or needs changing—eg. using fingers as words then touching the finger/word that is in need of correction)

6) Word Chart

(Words are depicted on charts, the sounds in each word corresponding in colour to the Sound-Colour Chart described above—students use this to build sentences)

7) Fidel Chart

(A chart that is colour-coded according to the sound-colour chart but includes the various English spellings so that they can be directly related to actual sounds)

8) Structured Feedback

(Students are invited to make observations about the day's lesson and what they have learned)

3.7. Suggestopedia

In the late 70s, a Bulgarian psychologist by the name of Georgi Lozanov introduced the contention that students naturally set up psychological barriers to learning—based on fears that they will be unable to perform and are limited in terms of their ability to learn. Lozanov believed that learners may have been using only 5 to 10 per cent of their mental capacity, and that the brain could process and retain much more material if given optimal conditions for learning. Based on psychological research on extrasensory perception, Lozanov began to develop a language learning method that focused on "desuggestion" of the limitations learners think they have, and providing the sort of relaxed state of mind that would facilitate the retention of material to its maximum potential. This method became known as Suggestopedia (but also—rather confusingly—Desuggestopedia)—the name reflecting the application of the power of "(de)suggestion" to the field of pedagogy.

One of the most unique characteristics of the method was the use of soft Baroque music during the learning process. Baroque music has a specific rhythm and a pattern of 60 beats per minute, and Lozanov believed it created a level of relaxed concentration that facilitated the intake and retention of huge quantities of material. This increase in learning potential was put down to the increase in alpha brain waves and decrease in blood pressure and heart rate that resulted from listening to Baroque music. Another aspect that differed from other methods to date was the use of soft comfortable chairs and dim lighting in the classroom (other factors believed to create a more relaxed state of mind).

Other characteristics of Suggestopedia were the giving over of complete control and authority to the teacher and the encouragement of learners to act as "childishly" as possible, often even assuming names and characters in the target language. All of these principles in combination were seen to make the students "suggestible", and therefore able to utilise their maximum mental potential to take in and retain new material.

The prime objective of Suggestopedia is to tap into more of students' mental potential to learn, in order to accelerate the process by which they learn to understand and use the target language for communication. Four factors considered essential in this process were the provision of a relaxed and comfortable learning environment, the use of soft Baroque music to help increase alpha brain waves and decrease blood pressure and heart rate, "desuggestion" in terms of the pyschological barriers learners place on their own learning potential, and "suggestibility" through the encouragement of learners assuming "child-like" and/or new roles and names in the target language.

3.7.1. Features

Here are some of the key features of Suggestopedia:

1) Learning is facilitated in an environment that is as comfortable as possible, featuring soft cushioned seating and dim lighting.
2) "Peripheral" learning is encouraged through the presence in the learning environment of posters and decorations featuring the target language and various grammatical information.
3) The teacher assumes a role of complete authority and control in the classroom.
4) Self-perceived and psychological barriers to learners' potential to learn are "desuggested".
5) Students are encouraged to be child-like, take "mental trips with the teacher" and assume new roles and names in the target language in order to become more "suggestible".
6) Baroque music is played softly in the background to increase mental relaxation and potential to take in and retain new material during the lesson.
(7) Students work from lengthy dialogues in the target language, with an accompanying translation into the students' native language.
8) Errors are tolerated, the emphasis being on content and not structure. Grammar and vocabulary are presented and given treatment from the teacher, but not dwelt on.
9) Homework is limited to students re-reading the dialogue they are studying—once before they go to sleep at night and once in the morning before they get up.
10) Music, drama and "the Arts" are integrated into the learning process as often as possible.

Some common/typical techniques closely associated with Suggestopedia as follows:

1) Classroom Set-up

   (Emphasis is placed on creating a physical environment that does not "feel" like a normal classroom, and makes the students feel as relaxed and comfortable as possible)

2) Peripheral Learning

   (Students can absorb information "effortlessly" when it is perceived as part of the environment, rather than the material "to be attended to")

3) Positive Suggestion

   (Teachers appeal to students' consciousness and subconscious in order to better orchestrate the "suggestive" factors involved in the learning situation)

4) Visualisation

   (Students are asked to close their eyes and visualise scenes and events, to help them relax, facilitate positive suggestion and encourage creativity from the students)

5) Choose a New Identity

   (Students select a target language name and/or occupation that places them "inside" the language they are learning)

6) Role-play

   (Students pretend temporarily that they are someone else and perform a role using the target language)

7) First Concert

   (Teacher does a slow, dramatic reading of the dialogue synchronised in intonation with classical music)

8) Second Concert

   (Students put aside their scripts and the teacher reads at normal speed according to the content, not the accompanying pre-Classical or Baroque music—this typically ends the class for the day)

9) Primary Activation

   (Students "playfully" reread the target language out loud, as individuals or in groups)

10) Secondary Activation

   (Students engage in various activities designed to help the students learn the material and use it more spontaneously—activities include singing, dancing, dramatisations and games—"communicative intent" and not "form" being the focus)

3.8. Total Physical Response Method

Already in the late 1800s, a French teacher of Latin by the name of Francois Gouin was hard at work devising a method of language teaching that capitalised on the way children naturally learn their first language, through the transformation of perceptions into conceptions and then the expression of those conceptions using language. His approach became known as the *Series Method,* involving direct conceptual teaching of language using series of inter-connected sentences that are simple and easy to perceive, because the language being used can be directly related to whatever the speaker is doing at the immediate time of utterance (ie, one's actions and language match each other). His thinking was well ahead of his time, and the Series Method became swamped in the enthusiasm surrounding the other new approach at the time in the form of the Direct Method.

One of the primary objectives of the TPR methodology was that learning needed to become more enjoyable and less stressful.

3.8.1. Features

Here are some of the key features of the Total Physical Response method:

1) The teacher directs and students "act" in response—"The instructor is the director of a stage play in which the students are the actors".
2) Listening and physical response skills are emphasized over oral production.
3) The imperative mood is the most common language function emplcyed, even well into advanced levels. Interrogatives are also heavily used.
4) Whenever possible, humour is injected into the lessons to make them more enjoyable for learners.
5) Students are not required to speak until they feel naturally ready or confident enough to do so.
6) Grammar and vocabulary are emphasized over other language areas. Spoken language is emphasized over written language.

Some common/typical techniques closely associated with TPR as follows:

1) Using Commands to Direct Behaviour

   (The use of commands requiring physical actions from the students in response is the major teaching technique)

2) Role Reversal

   (Students direct the teacher and fellow learners)

3) Action Sequence

   (Teacher gives interconnected directions which create a sequence of actions [also called an "operation"]—as students progress in proficiency, more and more commands are added to the action sequence. Most everyday activities can be broken down into a sequence of actions)

3.9. Natural Approach

Stephen Krashen and Tracy Terrell developed the Natural Approach in the early eighties, based on Krashen's theories about second language acquisition. As part of the Natural Approach, students listen to the teacher using the target language communicatively from the very beginning. It has certain similarities with the much earlier Direct Method, with the important exception that students are allowed to use their native language alongside the target language as part of the language learning process. In early stages, students are not corrected during oral production, as the teacher is focusing on meaning rather than form.

Communicative activities prevail throughout a language course employing the Natural Approach, focusing on a wide range of activities including games, roleplays, dialogues, group work and discussions. There are three generic stages identified in the approach: (1) Preproduction—developing listening skills; (2) Early Production—students struggle with the language and make many errors which are corrected based on content and not structure; (3) Extending Production—promoting fluency through a variety of more challenging activities.

3.10. Cognitive Approach

Cognitive theory assumes that responses are also the result of insight and intentional patterning. Insight can be directed to (a) the concepts behind language i.e. to traditional grammar. It can also be directed to (b) language as an operation—sets of communicative functions.

A variety of activities practised in new situations will allow assimilation of what has already been learnt or partly learnt. It will also create further situations for which existing language resources are inadequate and must accordingly be modified or extended—"accommodation". This ensures an awareness and a continuing supply of learning goals as well as aiding the motivation of the learner.

Trainers of English language teachers can achieve practical coverage of cognitive learning theory by reviewing the history of language teaching, especially the period in the mid 20th century when "meaningful drills" were being advocated and the shortcomings of "meaningless drills" were being highlighted. Although drilling and rote learning became subject to considerable prejudice in some educational circles in the late 20th century, no language learner will proceed very far without recognition of language structure and nobody will succeed in learning much without practice and repetition. Knowledge of the "types of drill" which the accomplished language teacher or informed computer learning programme can employ provide a full toolkit for anybody responsible for learning and teaching.

Another ploy often used by teacher trainers is to put trainee teachers into the situations encountered by language learners. This is often done through demonstrations where new languages (of which trainees have no knowledge) are presented. As homework students are often required to learn new languages to a basic level. It is hoped that they will be reminded of the problems, especially the conceptual ones. Often, there is not enough time to do this on short teacher training courses.

The aim of language practice drills is to train learners to talk and to help them master the basic structural patterns of the target language. As a method of language practice, drills are difficult to reconcile when the language becomes "meaningless".

The drawbacks of meaningless drills:

1. lack of context
2. failure to offer learner an element of discrimination or choice
3. failure to give rise to naturalistic speech
4. they fail grammatically in many instances.

Lack of context results from behaviourist principle of focusing uniquely on form: the one-step-at-a-time approach which attempts to forestall mistakes. Unique focus on form may succeed in the controlled environment, but the benefits of structural learning may not be transferred into the real environment. Drills attempting to forestall mistakes show only positive instances of what can be done. Negative instances are not given. The meaning conveyed by an utterance (e.g. I'm not going) is a matter of the function of the sentence as a whole in the larger context in which it occurs. A sentence does more than communicate information. It performs a role both in relation to other utterances that have been produced and as part of the interactive process involving the participants.

3.10.1. Meaningful Drills

In order to qualify as "meaningful", a drill must provide:

1. A context for the utterance it contains—without context, there is a risk of over-generalisation. "The meaning conveyed by an utterance is a matter of the function of the sentence (utterance) as a whole in the larger context in which it occurs.
2. It should give rise to naturalistic language
3. It should allow the learner some element of choice or discrimination.

3.10.2. Synonymy Drills

The role of repetition—a principle of both behaviourist and cognitive theories of learning. Regardless of preferences for behaviourist or cognitive, most teachers would find a place for repetition (for purposes of practice & consolidation), comparison (differentiation through minimal pairs or paired grammatical forms). The use of drills at different levels of language proficiency:

1. Drills are likely to be useful at elementary level or in the "practice phase" of a lesson where limitation of the learning goal is desirable.
2. Drills are likely to be useful at the intermediate level where practice, revision and checking of learning is particularly important.

3. Drills are likely to be useful at the advanced level to diagnose and iron out a particular difficulty.

Drills may be tried with the whole class or used on an individual basis, perhaps for remedial purposes. The limitations of drills are clearly matched by useful possibilities.

References

Asher, James, *Learning Another Language Through Actions: The Complete Teacher's Guidebook,* Los Gatos, CA: Sly Oaks Productions, 1977.

Brown, H. Douglas, *Teaching by Principles: An Interactive Approach to Language Pedagogy,* Prentice Hall, 1994.

Finocchiaro, Mary & Brumfit, Christopher, *The Functional-Notional Approach: From Theory to Practice,* Oxford University Press, 1983.

Krashen, Stephen D., & Terrell, Tracy D., *The Natural Approach: Language Acquisition in the Classroom,* Pergamon Press, 1983.

Larsen-Freeman, Dianne, *Techniques and Principles in Language Teaching,* New York: Oxford University Press, 1986.

Nunan, David, *Language Teaching Methodology: A Textbook for Teachers,* Prentice Hall, 1991.

Prator, Clifford H. & Celce-Murcia, Marianne, "An outline of language teaching approaches", In Celce-Murcia, Marianne & McIntosh, Lois (Ed.), *Teaching English as a Second or Foreign Language,* Newbury House, 1979.

Richards, Jack & Rodgers, Theodore, *Approaches and Methods in Language Teaching,* New York: Cambridge University Press, 1986.

4

Tools and Technologies in Teaching English

Technology, especially modern information and communication technology, holds great potential for significantly improving second language learning. Hence when faced with a technology (such as the radio), second language educators need to interpret its technological capacity in the terms of second language learning. In other words, educators must work out how this technology can be used to help enhance second language learning. This "figuring out" process is essentially a reinventing process that translates the capacities of a technology into a solution to a problem in the second language learning process. How a technology is used is the direct result of this translation process, which is affected by the translator's (educator's) understanding of the capacities of technology, which is inevitably constrained by the real functions of the technology, and her view of the educational goals and process, which is in turn influenced and limited by the context in which the learning occurs. The computer, for instance, when viewed as a tool for teachers, is used to address problems teachers face: communicating with their peers, students, and parents, record keeping, or preparing for classes. When viewed as a tool for the learner, the computer is then used to solve problems of the learner: accessing learning materials, completing homework, or obtaining feedback.

The power of technology only lies in its uses. And because the uses are the result of the user's interpretation guided by their knowledge of technological capacities, identification of problems, and thinking about the internal connection between the capacity and the problem, how the uses of each technology are conceptualised becomes one of the determining factors affecting the ultimate impact of technology. Traditional conceptualisation of technology uses in second language learning has a number of problems that have limited the impact of technology on second language acquisition.

First, it tends to focus on the potential uses of individual technologies instead of the combined potential of all technologies. Thus we see a large amount of individual software or hardware for language education but seldom see a comprehensive environment that integrates the capacities of multiple technologies to support language learning. For example, currently most language learning software is developed for the computer and thus can only be used when a computer is available, making it impossible for the learner to access the learning materials when he or she does not have access to a computer or is unable to use a computer. This is especially problematic for children from low-come or minority families.

Second, traditional conceptualisation of technology uses in second language learning tends to focus individual language learning issues instead of the learning process as a whole. Thus we see numerous individual tools and experiments that help with grammar, vocabulary, reading, or writing but rarely see a comprehensive design that coherently uses technology to help the learner with all aspects of learning. This is particularly true of uses of technology in formal language instruction.

Third, it tends to focus on newer technologies while ignoring older technologies. Thus we see repeated abandonment of promising uses of older technologies for newer technologies. Over the past century or so, we have seen multiple waves of attempts to use technology to support language learning: motion pictures, radios, televisions, main-frame computer systems, laser discs, CD ROMs, Hypermedia, and now the Internet. Each time a new technology emerged, it quickly replaced older technologies. Today, only a minority of language learning materials is available on and delivered with technologies other than the computer, with the exception of print-based technologies, which are of course rarely considered as technology any longer. The replacement of traditional audio-visual language labs with newer computer-based networked language learning centers is a telling example. It should be noted that some language learning materials are still available on audio cassette tapes, but the trend is certainly moving toward more digital technologies.

Lastly, existing research on technology for language learning tends to have focused on adult language learners. Thus we see much more research and development efforts for technology for adult language learners in instructional settings than for younger learners in the home environments. After an extensive review of the research literature of computer assisted language learning, concludes that: a) the settings of instruction where the studies were conducted were limited to higher education and adult learners, b) the languages studied were limited to common foreign languages and English as a foreign or second language, and c) the experiments were often short-term and about one or two aspects of language learning (e.g., vocabulary or grammar). Thus we need a new, more fruitful conceptualisation of how to use technology to enhance second language learning. This conceptualisation should aim to develop an effective language learning environment through technology instead of merely developing effective uses to support one aspect of language learning or making use of one type of technology. Furthermore, this conceptualisation should be grounded in second language acquisition research and focus on supporting the whole language learning process with all available technologies.

4.1. Effective Language Learning

Many language educators and researchers have been seeking ways to improve the quality of foreign/second language education. While there exists tremendous amount of disagreement about the specifics of an optimal language learning environment, research and practice seem to suggest that successful language learning can only occur when four conditions are met:

1) high quality input;
2) ample opportunities for practice;
3) high quality feedback; and
4) individualised content.

4.1.1. High Quality Input

The essential role of input remains unchallenged across different perspectives to second language acquisition, be it the dominant behaviourist perspective in the 70s or the current prevalent socio-cognitive perspective. The current approaches to second language acquisition, ranging from the universal grammar position to the input-interaction perspective, all embrace input as a necessary component, although they differ in their emphases on the type and amount of input that is considered crucial to triggering learning.

Simply put, a person, regardless of her age, cannot successfully learn a second or any language without sufficient exposure to authentic, diverse, comprehensible, and demanding linguistic and cultural materials of the target language. Second language acquisition researchers have invested much effort to theorise and empirically test the quality and quantity of input that are optimal to second language acquisition. Over the years, scholars have posited and investigated several qualities of input: comprehensible input, simplified input, modified input, and enhanced input. The stress of early research on input was to manipulate input in certain ways to facilitate learners' comprehension of the target language, and the current foci of research have shifted towards finding ways to make input presented in manners that draw learners' attention to certain linguistic forms and help them build form-meaning connections.

Modified input involved learners in active participation of the communication process and thus had the potential to enhance the possibility for learners to notice certain problematic linguistic forms. Enhanced input, in the form of text enhancement, input flooding and structured input, was put forth as a result of researchers' effort to find ways of manipulating input to draw learners' attention to certain linguistic forms, and help build form-meaning connections. The evolution of the construct input revolved around the understanding that input, though the driving force for language acquisition, could not guarantee learning, but rather needed to be processed to become intake so as to be integrated into learners' interlanguage system. Gass pointed out that selective attention was the core of this process and some important 'input filters' were external variables such as time available for processing the input, frequency of the input, affective factors and learners' prior knowledge, salience of forms as well as the linguistic information of the input itself. In another word, both variables external and internal to the learners are crucial if efforts were to be made to facilitate the input-to-intake process.

4.1.2. Communicative Opportunities for Practice

In addition to high-quality input, language learners must have ample opportunities to practice what they have been exposed. Thus communication has long been recognised as beneficial and essential to effective second language learning. Views of the role of communication have gone through drastic change in the past decades. For a long time communication had been acknowledged for practising what had been previously taught, and now it is touted as not only a "medium of practice" but the "means by which learning takes place" as well. Currently, the association between communication and learning is conceptualised and expounded in two major perspectives to second language learning: interactionist perspective and sociocultural perspective.

Sociocultural theory also makes a strong argument for the role of communication in second language learning. Sociocultural theory argues that any higher form of mental activities are mediated by symbolic means, language being one of the primary semiotic tool that humans used to mediate their cognitive processes, including language acquisition. Language mediates both social interactions on the "interpsychological plane" and thought on the "intrapsychological plane". Language learning is a mental activity that is carried out in the joint communication activity between experts and novices, with the former assisting the latter, using language as a major mediating tool. In other words, it is through social interactions, facilitated by language, that the learner or child internalises the external world or culture system, language being a major part of it. Social interactions must occur in certain cultural or social contexts. Thus authentic communications or dialogues also play a significant role in facilitating the acquisition of language in context.

4.1.3. High-Quality Feedback

Feedback is a classical concept in learning, whose importance is acknowledged across different learning theories. In the 60s, the heyday of behaviourism, feedback is viewed as a crucial component in the learning process, and is considered as the "conditioned connection of behaviour and reward". Cognitivism, placing learners at the center of the learning process, values feedback more for its informative function than for its corrective-reinforcing function and takes it as a channel to provide learners with information to assist them reach their objectives by reporting their mistakes to them. Situative theory stresses the necessity and centrality of social interaction in learning, and suggests that feedback is more often expressed in an interactive manner and serves as the core of social interaction that drives learning. Whatever perspectives on learning to adopt, it is widely accepted that feedback plays a crucial role in learning, second language learning without exception.

Research on feedback and second language learning has a long history, with early efforts on accounting for potential mistakes learners may make through contrastive analysis and on investigating learners' perceptions of feedback in second language learning. Positive feedback, confirmation of learners' language production as being acceptable in the target language, helps learners to strengthen linguistic knowledge already registered in their interlanguage system. Whereas negative feedback, an indication that certain features in learners' language production are impossible in the target language, serves more as a catalyst for the reconstruction of learners' interlanguage grammar and thus has attracted more research attention. Although there is still disagreement about whether negative feedback should be used in second language education because it may negatively affect the learner's motivation and discourage him from actively participating in authentic communications, it seems that most scholars agree, based on theoretical arguments and some empirical evidence, that negative or corrective feedback is in some instances a necessary condition for second language acquisition.

A growing body of research has examined how an interlocutor's negative feedback could promote second language learning. The negative feedback categorised into three types: explicit negative feedback (i.e., overt correction), implicit negative feedback in the form of communication breakdown (i.e., negotiation moves) and implicit negative feedback in the form of recast. In all, current research in second language acquisition confirmed the importance of the provision of feedback, negative feedback in particular, in facilitating second language learning. In addition, it suggested that a one-for-all solution or an ideal case for the provision of feedback does not exist and there is great necessity to vary the presentation of feedback to fit different learning conditions. Furthermore, it identified several important variables that need to be taken into consideration when providing feedback: the content of the feedback (specificity, length, etc.), individual differences, saliency and immediacy of feedback.

4.1.4. Individualised Content

Individual differences of the learner in terms of language proficiency, cognitive development, learning objectives, and learning styles are common and significant factors affecting learner motivation, language intake, and task performance. We know that not all language learners have the same linguistic aptitude. Some learn faster than others and some can reach a higher level of proficiency than others. In classroom situations, it is also possible that some learners may already have experiences with the target language while others in the same class may be true beginners. Language learners differ in their purposes for learning a second language. Some learn because they want to understand and experience a foreign language. Others want to communicate and conduct business in the target language with its native speakers. Some learn the language because they hope to live and work in the target culture, while others simply want to be able to read scientific and technical publications in the target language. It is thus unwise to force all students to be at the same level of competence in all aspects of the language—reading, listening, writing, and speaking.

Moreover, learners also differ in their learning styles and strategies. They have different approaches and strategies to learning grammar, vocabulary, and pronunciation. They also have different reading and listening strategies and they have different preferences for communicative settings. Lastly, learning occurs in different contexts. Some learners have more access to the target language at home while others may only have access in class. Some learners can spend more time on learning while others may not. Thus an effective language learning programme should be responsive to these individual differences and enable the learners to adjust the difficult level of the content, control the pace of learning, and select content that is appropriate for their own needs. In other words, the learning should be highly individualised and customisable in order to motivate all students, meet their diverse learning goals and styles, and accommodate their individual psychological and cognitive needs. Otherwise, the learners may not be able to benefit from the environment, fall behind, lose interest, and ultimately give up the learning. These four conditions are generally accepted and have been articulated by other scholars, although in slightly different language.

Translating these conditions into more specific actions, the ideal teacher or teaching system should be one that:

- Helps learners develop and elaborate their increasingly specified cognitive representation for the second language;
- Allows learners to experiment and take risks in a psychologically favourable and motivating environment;
- Offers input to both conscious and unconscious learning processes;
- Offers learners opportunities to practice and to receive feedback on performance;
- Allows learners to learn according to their own purposes and goals;
- Puts learners in touch with other learners;
- Promotes cultural and social learning;
- Promotes interactivity in learning and communication;
- Exposes the learner to appropriate contexts for learning;
- Expands the learner's 'zone of proximal development';
- Builds to learner independence.

However many language education programmes do not meet the above conditions. In instructed language learning situations, such an ideal teacher or teaching system is not always readily available. For instance, authentic, comprehensible, and engaging linguistic and cultural materials, spoken or written, are not always present for many language learners. In language classrooms, teachers are the main source of oral linguistic and cultural input. In order to provide appropriate authentic input, a teacher needs to be proficient in the target language. But such teachers are often in short supply. Even in the US, a country with tremendous linguistic diversity, there is a severe shortage of foreign language teachers. The situation can get even worse when more schools start to offer foreign language programmes. In other countries such as China and Japan, most English teachers are themselves not proficient in the language. The situation of written materials is not any better. Textbooks are often outdated and uninteresting to students.

Furthermore, in foreign language classrooms peer to peer communication in the target language is very limited, often mechanical and lacks authenticity, which makes it difficult for learners to sustain interest in the communication. Moreover, psychological and linguistic factors may prevent students from becoming truly engaged in real conversations in the target language. Similarly relevant and immediate feedback is not often available to language learners due to class sizes and the individual differences among students.

4.2. Creating an Optimal Language Learning Environment

There are many ways to conceive possible applications of technology in language education. A productive approach is to view it as a tool that enables the conditions for optimal language learning. Technology can be used to provide high quality input in a number of ways.

First, technology provides convenient access to a large variety of target language input via different media or combinations of media. Older technologies such as the TV, especially satellite TV, video and audio recorders/players, even films are effective means to bring authentic language and cultural materials to second language learners. It has been common practice for language teachers to use TV and radio programmes, movies, and other video and audio products in their classrooms. What has not been often considered often as potential technologies for enhancing language input is technology for entertainment such as video game consoles and DVD players. Somehow there exists a gigantic perceptual gap between technology for education and technology for entertainment. In fact, DVD players and video game consoles are very powerful platforms for delivering high-quality content, can also bring multimedia interactive content to the learner. They allow for more user control than traditional analog TVs and audio equipment. The multiple tracks of DVD technology can allow the learner to access input in a number of different ways: with or without captioning, in multiple languages, and or with or without commentaries. Newer technologies such as the Internet bring even more language resources.

A great number of resources in different languages are available free-of-charge on the Internet, and learners can get easy access to these authentic audio and/or visual materials. CMC, like email, online chat and video/audio conferencing, connects learners with native speakers and other learners and expands their exposure to various linguistic and cultural inputs. Hand-held digital devices, like MP3 players, and PDAs, allow learners to download Internet materials, both audio and textual, and have the information at their fingertips, thus enhancing the portability of these resources and freeing learners up from the physical constraints. E-books, with their manipulability (abilities to search and add audio conversion or short video annotation), the portability and the instant access, are available in a large collection of languages and offer both classical works and up-to-date reading materials.

Moreover, electronic highlighters, like QuickLink pen, allow learners to copy, clip and store printed text, Internet links, tables and charts and then transfer the data to their computers, PDAs or mobile phones, or translate the text into different languages or look up its meaning from a built-in dictionary. In all, current technology not only exposes learners to unprecedented large amount of input of great variety, but provides a lot of flexibility and convenience in the access, manipulation and organisation of the information.

Second, technology lends itself to easy and quick configuration of comprehensible and enhanced input so as to increase its possibility of being processed and integrated. For one thing, text enhancement, either visual or audio, could be easily conditioned using technologies with highlighting functions as simple as Microsoft Word and more complicated technologies that enable interactive features. For another, technology could also simplify input through complementing it with translations, textual or visual annotations, and elaborated information through hyperlinks. Concordancer is one such technology that generates lists of any given word/phrase used in various contexts, which is beneficial to the exploration of the use and meanings of specific linguistic items. Moreover, some concordance software even allows across language comparison allows up to four languages to be analysed in parallel and others provide corpus of language in a certain area.

Third, the edge of technology in appealing to different learning styles and proffering individualised input could tap the learner internal variables that are crucial to the input-to-intake process. Multimedia software as well as most online materials delivered via a combination of different media caters to learners with different cognitive styles. Technology also helps to lower affective filters: input provided in the form of games or simulations taps the fun component of learning; hypertext allows self-selected path of navigation and make input more individualised and personally meaningful. The flexibility and learner control offered by technology enable learners to choose linguistic input that fits their needs at their own pace, which would, to a great extent, enhance the possibility the incorporation of input into their interlanguage system.

4.2.1. Evidence of Effectiveness

Technology can be used to effectively enhance language learning through the provision of high quality input. Technology can be used to enhance the quality of input in the following ways:

- Enhancing access efficiency through digital multimedia technologies. Digital multimedia technologies were used to make access to learning materials more efficiently than print media or audio recorders because a) multimedia (visual, audio, and text) presentations can create stronger memory links than a single medium alone and b) digital technology allows instant and accurate playbacks, which helps the learner to access specific segments much more easily without spending time to locate them, which can be tedious and a waste of time.
- Enhancing authenticity using video and the Internet. Video materials can bring natural and context-rich linguistic and

cultural materials to the learner while the Internet enables the learner to access authentic news and literature in the target language, which can reflect current cultural changes more effectively than printed sources and more motivation.

- Enhancing comprehensibility through learner control and multimedia annotations. Comprehensible input is necessary for language learning but useful learning materials must also contain enough unfamiliar materials. For language learners, especially beginning and intermediate ones, authentic materials are often beyond their language proficiency and may become incomprehensible without help. To enhance comprehensibility of spoken materials, full caption, keyword caption, or slow-down the speech rate have been found to be effective found that the college ESL students who were able to flexibly slow down or speed up the rate of speech had significantly better listening comprehension than those who did not. For reading materials, glossing or multimedia annotations have been effective means to enhance comprehension.

4.2.2. Computer Mediated Communication

Engaging in authentic communication in the target language is another essential condition for successful language learning yet such opportunities do not exist for most learners. Technology can be used in many different ways to create opportunities for language learners to communicate in the target language. Currently, the most prevalent use of technology in this regard is computer mediated communication (CMC). CMC has been theorised as a crucial means to realise interactivity in online teaching and learning environments and promote a 'learnercentered interactive approach,' and to lead to the awareness of the sociocultural nature of the target language and the development of situated cognition.

Existing CMC software or systems can be classified into two major categories: synchronous systems and asynchronous systems. Synchronous CMC includes text-based conferencing systems (e.g., English clubchat; ICQ), audio-based conferencing systems (Netscape CoolTalk; StudyCom), video-based conferencing systems, and combinations thereof (MSN messenger; iVisit; PalTalk, etc.). Most current synchronous CMC systems provide all the three modalities, with varying degree of anonymity and user control . In addition, there're also some virtual reality (graphic-enhanced) conferencing systems available, such as The Palace and Active Worlds. These 2-D or 3-D systems allow learners to choose their own avatars, move about freely in the virtual worlds, and create their own virtual spaces and activities such as playing online games, shopping and making friends with people. Differing from synchronous CMC, asynchronous CMC provides communications free of time constraints. The majority of asynchronous CMC are text-based and in various forms: email, listserv, and threaded messages, such as discussion board and web forum. However, audio-based asynchronous CMC is also available, such as voice mail (e.g., HandyBits VoiceMail), which enables learners to send voice messages to each other using their email accounts. Another emerging asynchronous CMC is in the form of weblogs.

In recent years, the increased capacity of mobile phones and the convergence of phone systems and the Internet, plus the decreased cost and broadened accessibility have made mobile phones a viable technology-mediated communication tool for second language learners. With easy text-messaging, multimedia interactivities, and interoperability with the Internet, mobile phones can practically be used as networked computers. Thus many of the CMC functions can be performed with the mobile phones. Another way technology helps to facilitate communication is through supporting learner talk around technology-based activities. Ideally any kind of technology-based activities, such as watching a sit-com on the TV, searching for information on the Internet, creating PowerPoint presentation on a certain topic, playing instructional software, games or simulations, could be used in manners to stimulate learner talk.

The other noteworthy application of technology in promoting learner communication is human-computer interaction, talking with artificial intelligence agent to be specific. This area is least explored in regard to its efficacy in second language learning due to the fact that the technology in this function is still under development and has not been widely applied yet. However, the potential of this application in second language learning is tremendous. One potential use of the technology is chatterbot or bot, a conversation simulator based on artificial intelligence technology and is programmed to conduct conversations with users on various topics. The potential use of chatterbot in language learning is immense: it provides a convenient chatting environment for learners to conduct authentic conversations in the target language either by writing or by speaking, and the chat transcripts in the archives could serve as a source of the target language.

4.2.3. Using the Blackboard in Classroom

The blackboard continues to be a very important teaching aid throughout the world. The blackboard offers a variety of functions to the teachers of TESOL. You may use it to write the sentences, words and phrases you wish to teach. You may use it to test what the students have learned. You may use it to illustrate the meaning of words, phrases and sentences. You can invite your students to come forward and write what they have learned. So, it is important that you train yourself to use the blackboard effectively in your class.

1. Some teachers hide the board. And if the teacher has her back to the class she cannot control what the students are doing.
2. You need to keep eye contact with the class as you write. You should allow the class to see what you write.
3. You should keep the students' attention by saying the words as you write them.
4. Write clearly. The writing should be large enough to read from the back of the class.
5. Write in straight lines. This is easy if you only write across a section of the board, not across the whole board.
6. Talk as you write.
7. The blackboard should not be too crowded.
8. Choose only those items that need special and focused attention to write on the blackboard.
9. Write the key vocabulary down the side of the board, with similar items close together.

10. An important use of the blackboard is to show clearly how the structures are formed, and to show the differences between structures: He played football: Did he play football?
11. Use the blackboard to discuss how the students could make the structures. This could be done by underlining the important features.
12. You could use different coloured chalk (red, and green stand out most clearly).
13. You could draw arrows or write numbers to show the change in word order.
14. You can ask different students to come to the front in turn and present each set of examples on the blackboard.
15. Many teachers use the blackboard only for writing. But simple pictures drawn on the blackboard can help to increase the interest of a lesson, and are often a good way of showing meaning and conveying situations to the class.
16. Blackboard drawings should be as simple as possible, showing only the most important details. Very simple line drawings and stick figures, which are easy to draw.
17. It is important to draw quickly, so as to keep the interest of the class. Talk as you draw.
18. Simple blackboard drawings: Faces. Heads should be large enough to be seen from the back of the class. Show how you can indicate expression, especially by changing the shape of the mouth.
19. Show other expressions, for example, surprise by raised eyebrows, anger by a frown.
20. Show which way the speaker is facing by changing the nose. This is is useful if you want to show two people having a conversation.
21. Show sex or age by drawing hair.
22. Stick figures Show/draw basic male and female stick figures. The body should be about twice as long as the head; the arms are the same length as the body; the legs are slightly longer.

23. Indicate actions by bending the legs and arms.
24. Places. Show buildings, towns, and directions by a combination of pictures and words.
25. Vehicles. Draw vehicles and indicate movement.
26. Use blackboard drawings to build up a complete situation. This might be done to introduce a topic and new vocabulary, or as a preparation for reading a text or dialogue. Draw a school, then draw a boy running, then rub out the boy, and draw him again by the school, then draw another diagram with the boy and the teacher.
27. A series or sequence of pictures would tell the story better. Use the pictures as cues to students to tell the story.

4.2.4. Using English in Classroom

As much as possible, English should be used in your class from the beginning itself. This means that you will use English as frequently as possible for interaction with the students, and that you will ask students to use English as much as they can to express their personal needs and to engage themselves in conversations with you. Use English mainly in the activities below:

1. Introducing the lesson.
2. Checking attendance.
3. Organising where students sit.
4. Presenting new vocabulary.
5. Introducing a text.
6. Asking questions on a text.
7. Correcting errors.
8. Setting homework.

Note that in the initial stages you need to use a lot of gestures along with English to make the students understand what you wish to communicate to them. Sometimes you may be required to use the native language of your learners, or a language known to them as well as you. There are two main ways in which English can be used in class. It can be used in teaching the lesson itself: giving examples, introducing a text, asking questions, etc. It can also be used for activities which surround the lesson, but which are not actually part of the teaching: checking attendance, telling students where to sit, chatting students, controlling the class, etc.

There is great value in using English in class. If the teacher uses English most of the time, it will give the students practice in listening and responding to spoken English. This will help them pick up words and expressions beyond the language of the textbook. In the lesson itself, the language used is often unnatural and artificial. This will be modified to give an opportunity for real, natural English to be used. However, you should not feel that you must use English all the time. There are occasions when it can be useful to use the students' own language.

Use of English in the classroom is greatly facilitated through socialising conversations. Instead of going straight to the textbook at the beginning of a lesson, the teacher can spend a few minutes chatting to the class about topics of interest. Note that if you make use of English in natural conversation, it would amount to exposing your students to native speakers' English. Try to keep to simple language that you might use in your own class. You can talk and ask questions, but get the students to give only short responses. You can prompt individual students to talk more about things they have done. You can get students to talk and ask questions. Chatting creates an opportunity for real language practice, and creates an English language atmosphere in the class. Students get to know one another well. They come to know each other's names, and make small talks.

Even more important, it establishes contact with the class, and helps students to feel relaxed and ready to learn. Teachers have to say so many things simply to organise the lesson – starting or stopping an activity, getting students to do or not to do things. Much of this language consists of simple commands and instructions which are repeated lesson after lesson. If you say these in English, students will quickly learn what they mean. The following are some simple classroom commands in English, which you should continually use in your class:

— Stand up (please).
— Sit down (please).
— Look! Look at me.
— Listen!

- Repeat!
- Again! Open/Close your books.
- Stop talking!
- Come here, please.
- Come to the front.
- Be quiet, please.

Most of the language we need for organising the class consists of simple expressions which can be used again and again. However, teachers may often need to use more complex language, for example, when explaining a new word or a grammar point, or explaining how an activity works. In such instances also, make your explanations as simple and clear as possible, so that the students understand. Use simple, short sentences; use gestures to show each of the action you want them to understand. Use simple blackboard drawings; give difficult words in the language known to the students. Giving explanations in English is worthwhile if it can be done successfully and without too much difficulty. However, there are many occasions when it is best to use the students' own language—either because the language needed is too complex, or because it is easier, quicker, and more convenient.

An explanation in English could be very confusing, especially if the concept or words are unfamiliar to the students. It would be better to give examples in English, and then to give a translation of the word. By using the students' own language, we can give a clearer and fuller explanation, and refer to equivalent expressions in their language. It is best not to rely only on explanations in either language. It is more important to give plenty of examples and a chance for students to practice. An advantage of using the students' own language is that the situation can be given more quickly and easily, leaving more time for practice. However, an advantage of using English is that it provides useful listening practice, and helps students by giving them some of the words they need.

4.2.5. Using Visuals

Visual aids include pictures, objects, and things for the students to look at and talk about. Visual aids are important because showing visuals focuses attention on meaning, and helps to make the language in the class more real and alive; having something to look at keeps the students' attention, and makes the class more interesting; visuals can be used at any stage of the lesson, to help in presenting new language or introducing a topic, as part of language practice, and when reviewing language that has been presented earlier; good visual aids can be used again and again and shared by different teachers.

You can use the following as visual aids in your class: yourself, the blackboard, real objects, flashcards, pictures, and charts. The teacher can use gestures, facial expressions, and actions to help show the meaning of words and to illustrate situations. You can use the blackboard to draw pictures, diagrams, maps, etc. You can use real objects in the classroom and bring other things into the class – food, clothes, containers, household objects, vegetables, etc.

Flashcards with single pictures can be held up by the teacher in the class. These can be used for presenting and practising new words and structures, and for revision. The teacher can draw a picture on the flashcard, or stick on a picture from magazine. Flashcards can also be used to show words or numbers. Charts are large sheets of card or paper with writing, pictures or diagrams, used for more extended presentation or practice. These may be displayed on the wall or blackboard.

The Fleming System dictates that all people systematically go through the same sequence of events in order to comprehend a visual image. First, a given learner recalls, recognises, acknowledges and reproduces a mental picture of the visual input. Second, the learner goes through an analytic period. It is at this point that the learner attempts to separate, identify, and compare the components of the illustration. This includes assessing, judging, describing and/or identifying components of the desired image. The next stage finds the learner trying to combine components, formulate new relationships and generalise information based on the input. In the application stage, the learner attempts to "apply" the visual to a situation. Finally researchers hypothesise that the learner demonstrates a desired interest in the visual.

A visual is any projected or non-projected image that can be classified into illustrations, visuals, pictures, perceptions, mental images, figures, impressions, likeness, replicas, reproductions or anything that would help a learner see an immediate meaning. The visual is considered projected when it is planned for and executed with an intended meaning. In contrast, the non-projected visual is the result of an spontaneous occurance of an image that is usually unplanned and occurs in relationship as a result of a triggered catalyst.

Learners prefer visuals that are coloured, contain a story, relate to previous experiences and that can be associated with places, objects, persons, events or animals of which they are familiar. Likewise, it has also shown that if a visual stimulus is suddenly terminated that it remains available in the conscious system only for about a second in detail. Moreover, learners prefer time when comprehending a visual. For example, when a given visual is flashed with time for comprehension and/or is masked with another visual that recognition for the learner can be impaired.

To use visuals in the context of language learning. One must subscribe to the following assumptions:

1. Imagery can facilitate learning.
2. Imagery (combined with the use of texts) make subjects more likely to think about the process of the language more fully.
3. Imagery may hinder language learning. For example, imagery has been known to interfere with performance in various concurrent visual tasks.

A learner's sensitivity to language and their ability to create relations amongst words can be further enhanced by the use of visuals. Graphic images can bring out more detailed, knowledgeable, responsive, awareness to the object, situation or text being communicated. Moreover, the use of a picture may lead a learner to more abstract thought as well as the ability to distinguish ideas or to demonstrate greater precision counting organising skills through the use of logical structure. Overall, an bring out a more complex sensitivity in the learner.

Pictures help individual learners predict information, infer information, deduce information, analyse today's world so that it can be brought into today's classroom and offer social settings which can immerse or expose the learner to new ideas or further promote an already created setting. If a visual is used in a testing or teaching situation it can enhance clarity and give meaning to the text or to the message being communicated. Visuals can serve to create a solid link between the material learned and the practical application of it on a test.

The nature of a graphic images serves as a catalyst and stimulus. Moreover, the visual can offer input, output and/or feedback on materials learned. Likewise, a learner using a visual may be more apt to give an added response to the traditionally expected form. The response may change according to the picture in collaboration with the task as it works as an interactive negotiator. Although some practitioners may argue that a picture can serve as an impetus, others would equally argue that the same picture has the potential to urge an opinion. As teachers manipulate texts daily in lessons, teachers can also control and open a picture to a variety of language learning activities as well as a variety of interpretations.

Visuals allow for greater cognitive mapping and navigating in an environment. The use of visuals can either lead to sensory acuteness or to sensory depravation. In the process, perception becomes the ability to process the stimuli as meaningful to the viewer. Visuals are a good and useful tool for examination purposes because they lead the learner into drawing out language from their own knowledge and personal experiences through exposure to, immersion to the stimuli presented before them. Visuals permit strategies to organise knowledge into semantic or associative clusters. In testing and teaching situations pictures items can be developed to test whether the students understands the syntax or structure of the target language.

Visuals allow for options, responses alternatives patterns and ranges. Students can see immediate meaning in terms of vocabulary recognition provided the item exists in the first language. Pictures can be developed into a test to see whether the learner understands the structure and the syntax. The advantages of pictures suggest that visuals can help make a task or situation more authentic. Pictures can help testers and teachers to identify or manipulate structures, vocabulary, functions, situations and skills. Visuals used as testing prompts can be used to measure semantic and associative clusters. Pictures allow students to focus on the whole item or a piece of an item. Pictures can give or not give a context depending on what needs to be tested. Pictures offer test takers options for more interpretive responses, patterns and ranges to answer posited exam questions.

Visual testing and teaching prompts can aid in measuring syntactical, phonological, lexical and cultural proficiency. Perhaps this is because a visual cue may also be accompanied by a written cue to focus a students' attention on the specific lexical unit being furnished. Pictures can force full or partial student production. For example, Visuals may possibly be able to empower test takers to decode information using top-down or bottom-up processes. Top down encoding in the visual process would include the learner testing ideas against facts or solving specific problems by viewing concept maps to relate their ideas to facts or ideas found in a second language text or test. In contrast, bottom up encoding in the visual process would include using the visual image to help learners to scan, sort and/or organise information in a testing environment.

The use of visual stimuli enables a learner and/or test-taker the ability to predict information, to infer information as well as to deduce information from the picture or mental image. Another beneficial reason for using pictures on examinations is authenticity. Visuals can bring today's world into the language learning environment by serving as an reflection of what exists outside of the foreign or second language classroom. This form of stimuli can allow the learner to analyse his/her own world. Visual stimuli can expose as well as immerse the test-taker into a familiar or unfamiliar environment, social setting or practical environment.

4.2.6. Computer-Assisted Language Learning (CALL)

Computer-assisted language learning (CALL) is a form of computer-based accelerated learning which carries two important features: bidirectional learning and individualised learning. It is not a method. CALL materials are tools for learning. The focus of CALL is learning, and not teaching. CALL materials are used in teaching to facilitate the language learning process. It is a student-centered accelerated learning material, which promotes self-paced accelerated learning. CALL originates from CAI (Computer-Accelerated Instruction), a term that was first viewed as an aid for teachers. The philosophy CALL emphasizes more on student-centered lessons allowing the learners to learn on their own using structured and/or unstructured interactive lessons. These lessons carry two important features: bidirectional (interactive) learning and individualised learning. CALL is not a method. It is a tool that helps teachers to facilitate language learning process. CALL can be used to reinforce what has been learned in the classrooms. It can also be used as remedial to help learners with limited language proficiency.

The design of CALL lessons generally takes into consideration principles of language pedagogy, which may be derived from learning theories (behaviourist, cognitive, and constructivist) and second language learning such as Krashen's Monitor Theory. CALL can be made independent of the Internet. It can stand alone for example in a CDROM format. Depending on its design and objectives, it may include a substantial interactive element especially when CALL is integrated in web-based format. It may include the search for and the investigation of applications in language teaching and learning. Except for self-study software, CALL is meant to supplement face-to-face language instruction, not replace it.

4.2.6.1. Technologies used in CALL instruction

The technologies used in CALL instruction generally fall into two categories, software and Internet-based activities.

Software

Authoring programmes allow an instructor to programme part or all of the content to be learned and programme part or all of how the content is to be learned. Some examples of these programmes include Hotpotatoes, WinCALIS, Clozemaster, Choicemaster and Multitester. With these, the format is pre-programmed and the instructor puts in the material. General authoring programmes like Macromedia Director can be used to make an entire course; however, most teachers do not have the time or the technical ability to make use of such programmes.

A courseware used in a CALL environment can be designed specifically for foreign/second language learning or adapted for this purpose. Most language textbook publishers offer educational software of some sort, whether it is meant to support a paper textbook or to stand alone for self-study.

Most programmes designed for language learning are tutorials. These generally are drill programmes that consist of a brief introduction plus a series of questions to which the learner responds and then the computer gives some kind of feedback. With these kinds of programmes, the material to be learned may already be programmed in by the publisher, which is more common, or may allow the teacher to programme in the material to be learned. Yet, there are also integrated CALL programmes, especially web-based CALL programmes that combine tutorials, exercises (interactive multimedia drill-practice lessons), tests, and language enrichment materials. In fact, the site, where multimedia CALL lessons are offered, may also include e-forum and chat for the language learners to extend their learning process in a more dynamic atmosphere.

Internet-based

The World Wide Web was launched in 1992 reaching the general public by 1993, opening up new possibilities in CALL. Internet activities vary considerably, from online versions of software (where the learner interacts with a networked computer), to computer-mediated communication (where the learner interacts with other people via the computer), to applications that combine these two elements. Nowadays, websites that cater to foreign-language learners, especially those learning English, are so numerous and varied that it can be very difficult to determine where to begin.

Computer-managed communication (CMC) has been around in one form or another since the 1960's but only became widely available to the general public since the early 1990's. CMC comes in two basic forms: asynchronous, such as email and forums, and synchronous, such as text chat, voice chat and audio- and video-conferencing. With such facilities learners can communicate in the target language with other real speakers cheaply, 24 hours a day. Learners can communicate one-to-one or one-to-many as well as sharing audio and video files. Because of all this, CMC has had a considerable impact on language teaching. Special interest groups, such as the EUROCALL CMC SIG have been set up to further the use of CMC in language learning and teaching.

4.2.6.2. CALL and Computational Linguistics

CALL and computational linguistics are separate but somewhat interdependent fields of study. The basic goal of computational linguistics is to "teach" computers to generate and comprehend grammatically-acceptable sentences... for purposes of translation and direct communication with computers where the computer understands and generates natural language. Computational linguistics takes the principles of theoretical linguistics with the aim of characterising a language with computational applications in mind.

A very simple example of computers understanding natural language in relation to second language learning is vocabulary drill exercises. The computer "understands" the input word by comparing it with a stored answer and gives feedback to the user. On a superficial level, the core issue for humans and computers using language is the same; finding the best match between a given speech sound and it corresponding word string, then generating the correct and appropriate response. However, humans and machines process speech in fundamentally different ways. Humans use complex cognitive processes, taking into account variables such as social situations and rules while speech for a computer is simply a series of digital values to generate and parse language. For this reason, those involved in CALL from a computational linguistics perspective tend to be more optimistic about a computer's ability to do error analysis and other pedagogical tasks than those who come into CALL via language teaching.

4.2.6.3. Theoretical Basis for CALL Instruction Design

Computers have become so widespread in schools and homes and their uses have expanded so dramatically that the majority of language teachers now think about the implications. Technology brings about changes in the teaching methodologies of foreign language unless they are used simply to automate fill-in-the-gap exercises. The use of the computer in and of itself does not constitute a teaching method, but rather the computer forces pedagogy to think in new ways to exploit the computers benefits and work around its limitations. To exploit computers' potential we need language teaching specialists who can promote a complementary relationship between computer technology and appropriate pedagogic programmes.

A number of pedagogical approaches have developed in the computer age, including the communicative and integrative/ experimentative approaches. Others include constructivism, whole language theory and sociocultural theory although they are not exclusively theories of language learning. With constructivism, students are active participants in a task in which they "construct" new knowledge based on experience in order to incorporate new ideas into their already-established schema of knowledge. Whole language theory postulates that language learning (either native or second language) moves from the whole to the part; rather than building sub-skills like grammar to lead toward higher abilities like reading comprehension, whole language insists the opposite is the way we really learn to use language. Students learn grammar and other sub-skills by making intelligent guesses bases on the input they have experienced. It also promotes that the four skills (reading, writing, listening and speaking) are interrelated. Sociocultural theory states that learning is a process of becoming part of a desired community and learning that communities rules of behaviour.

4.3. Changing Roles for Teachers and Students

Although the integration of CALL into a foreign language programme can lead to great anxiety among language teachers, researchers consistently claim that CALL changes, sometimes radically, the role of the teacher but does not eliminate the need for a teacher altogether. Instead of handing down knowledge to students and being the center of students' attention, teachers become guides as they construct the activities students are to do and help them as students complete the assigned tasks. In other words, instead of being directly involved in students' constructions of the language, the teacher interacts with students primarily to facilitate difficulties in using the target language (grammar, vocabulary, etc.) as use the language to interact with the computer and/or other people.

Elimination of a strong teacher presence has been shown to lead to larger quantity and better quality of communication such as more fluidity, more use of complex sentences and more sharing of students' personal selves. However, teacher presence is still very important to students when doing CALL activities. Teachers should be familiar enough with the resources to be used to anticipate technical problems and limitations. Students need the reassuring and motivating presence of a teacher in CALL environments. Not only are they needed during the initial learning curve, they are needed to conduct review sessions to reinforce what was learned. Encouraging students to participate and offering praise are deemed important by students. Most students report preferring to do work in a lab with a teacher's or tutor's presence rather than completely on their own.

Students, too, need to adjust their expectations of their participation in the class in order to use CALL effectively. Rather than passively absorbing information, learners must negotiate meaning and assimilate new information through interaction and collaboration with someone other than the teacher, be that person a classmate or someone outside of the classroom entirely. Learners must also learn to interpret new information and experiences on their own terms. However, because the use of technology redistributes teachers' and classmates' attentions, less-able students can become more active participants in the class because class interaction is not limited to that directed by the teacher. Moreover more shy students can feel free in their own students'-centered environment. This will raise their self-esteem and their knowledge will be improving. If students are performing collaborative project they will do their best to perform it within set time limits.

References

Canning, C., "Visual Perception and Language Learning", *TESOL Arabia News*, 6:1, November 1998.

_______________ ., "Visual support and language teaching", *TESOL Arabia News*, Volume 5:4, March 1998.

Chapelle C., *Computer applications in second language acquisition: foundations for teaching, testing and research*, Cambridge: Cambridge University Press, 2001.

de Szendeffy J., *A practical guide to using computers in language teaching,* Ann Arbor: University of Michigan Press, 2005.

Jarvis H., "Technology and change in English Language Teaching (ELT)", *The Asian EFL Journal,* 2005.

Mitchell, R; F. Myles, *Second Language Learning Theories,* London: Arnold, 1998.

Ravichandran, T., *Computer-assisted language learning (CALL) in the perspective of the interactive approach: Advantages and apprehensions,* 2000.

Son J.-B. (ed.), *Computer Assisted Language Learning: concepts, contexts and practices,* Lincoln, NE: iUniverse, 2004.

Traynor, Patrick, "Effects of computer-assisted instruction on different learners", *Journal of Instructional Psychology,* July 2003.

Warschauer Mark, *Computer Assisted Language Learning: an Introduction,* 2008.

5

Teaching to Speak English Effectively

In the communicative model of language teaching, instructors help their students develop the ability to produce grammatically correct, logically connected sentences that are appropriate to specific contexts, and to do so using acceptable (that is, comprehensible) pronunciation.

5.1. Techniques for Teaching Speaking

The goal of teaching speaking skills is communicative efficiency. Learners should be able to make themselves understood, using their current proficiency to the fullest. They should try to avoid confusion in the message due to faulty pronunciation, grammar, or vocabulary, and to observe the social and cultural rules that apply in each communication situation. To help students develop communicative efficiency in speaking, instructors can use a balanced activities approach that combines language input, structured output, and communicative output.

Language input comes in the form of teacher talk, listening activities, reading passages, and the language heard and read outside of class. It gives learners the material they need to begin producing language themselves. Language input may be content oriented or form oriented.

- Content-oriented input focuses on information, whether it is a simple weather report or an extended lecture on an academic topic. Content-oriented input may also include descriptions of learning strategies and examples of their use.
- Form-oriented input focuses on ways of using the language: guidance from the teacher or another source on

vocabulary, pronunciation, and grammar (linguistic competence); appropriate things to say in specific contexts (discourse competence); expectations for rate of speech, pause length, turn-taking, and other social aspects of language use (sociolinguistic competence); and explicit instruction in phrases to use to ask for clarification and repair miscommunication (strategic competence).

In the presentation part of a lesson, an instructor combines content-oriented and form-oriented input. The amount of input that is actually provided in the target language depends on students' listening proficiency and also on the situation. For students at lower levels, or in situations where a quick explanation on a grammar topic is needed, an explanation in English may be more appropriate than one in the target language.

Structured output focuses on correct form. In structured output, students may have options for responses, but all of the options require them to use the specific form or structure that the teacher has just introduced. Structured output is designed to make learners comfortable producing specific language items recently introduced, sometimes in combination with previously learned items. Instructors often use structured output exercises as a transition between the presentation stage and the practice stage of a lesson plan. Textbook exercises also often make good structured output practice activities.

In *communicative output*, the learners' main purpose is to complete a task, such as obtaining information, developing a travel plan, or creating a video. To complete the task, they may use the language that the instructor has just presented, but they also may draw on any other vocabulary, grammar, and communication strategies that they know. In communicative output activities, the criterion of success is whether the learner gets the message across. Accuracy is not a consideration unless the lack of it interferes with the message.

In everyday communication, spoken exchanges take place because there is some sort of information gap between the participants. Communicative output activities involve a similar real information gap. In order to complete the task, students must reduce or eliminate the information gap. In these activities, language is a tool, not an end in itself. In a balanced activities approach, the teacher uses a variety of activities from these different categories of input and output. Learners at all proficiency levels, including beginners, benefit from this variety; it is more motivating, and it is also more likely to result in effective language learning.

5.2. Developing Speaking Skills

Students often think that the ability to speak a language is the product of language learning, but speaking is also a crucial part of the language learning process. Effective instructors teach students speaking strategies—using minimal responses, recognising scripts, and using language to talk about language—that they can use to help themselves expand their knowledge of the language and their confidence in using it. These instructors help students learn to speak so that the students can use speaking to learn.

5.2.1. Using Minimal Responses

Language learners who lack confidence in their ability to participate successfully in oral interaction often listen in silence while others do the talking. One way to encourage such learners to begin to participate is to help them build up a stock of minimal responses that they can use in different types of exchanges. Such responses can be especially useful for beginners. Minimal responses are predictable, often idiomatic phrases that conversation participants use to indicate understanding, agreement, doubt, and other responses to what another speaker is saying. Having a stock of such responses enables a learner to focus on what the other participant is saying, without having to simultaneously plan a response.

5.2.2. Recognising Scripts

Some communication situations are associated with a predictable set of spoken exchanges—a script. Greetings, apologies, compliments, invitations, and other functions that are influenced by social and cultural norms often follow patterns or scripts. So do the transactional exchanges involved in activities such as obtaining information and making a purchase. In these scripts, the relationship between a speaker's turn and the one that follows it can often be anticipated. Instructors can help students develop speaking ability by making them aware of the scripts for different situations so that they can predict what they will hear and what they will need to say in response. Through interactive activities, instructors can give students practice in managing and varying the language that different scripts contain.

5.2.3. Using Language to talk About Language

Language learners are often too embarrassed or shy to say anything when they do not understand another speaker or when they realise that a conversation partner has not understood them. Instructors can help students overcome this reticence by assuring them that misunderstanding and the need for clarification can occur in any type of interaction, whatever the participants' language skill levels. Instructors can also give students strategies and phrases to use for clarification and comprehension check. By encouraging students to use clarification phrases in class when misunderstanding occurs, and by responding positively when they do, instructors can create an authentic practice environment within the classroom itself. As they develop control of various clarification strategies, students will gain confidence in their ability to manage the various communication situations that they may encounter outside the classroom.

5.2.4. Speaking Activities

Traditional classroom speaking practice often takes the form of drills in which one person asks a question and another gives an answer. The question and the answer are structured and predictable, and often there is only one correct, predetermined answer. The purpose of asking and answering the question is to demonstrate the ability to ask and answer the question. In contrast, the purpose of real communication is to accomplish a task, such as conveying a telephone message, obtaining information, or expressing an opinion. In real communication, participants must manage uncertainty about what the other person will say. Authentic communication involves an information gap; each participant has information that the other does not have. In addition, to achieve their purpose, participants may have to clarify their meaning or ask for confirmation of their own understanding.

To create classroom speaking activities that will develop communicative competence, instructors need to incorporate a purpose and an information gap and allow for multiple forms of expression. However, quantity alone will not necessarily produce competent speakers. Instructors need to combine structured output activities, which allow for error correction and increased accuracy, with communicative output activities that give students opportunities to practice language use more freely.

5.2.4.1. *Structured Output Activities*

Two common kinds of structured output activities are *information gap* and *jigsaw* activities. In both these types of activities, students complete a task by obtaining missing information, a feature the activities have in common with real communication. However, information gap and jigsaw activities also set up practice on specific items of language. In this respect they are more like drills than like communication.

5.2.4.2. *Communicative Output Activities*

Communicative output activities allow students to practice using all of the language they know in situations that resemble real settings. In these activities, students must work together to develop a plan, resolve a problem, or complete a task. The most common types of communicative output activity are *role plays* and *discussions* .

In role plays, students are assigned roles and put into situations that they may eventually encounter outside the classroom. Because role plays imitate life, the range of language functions that may be used expands considerably. Also, the role relationships among the students as they play their parts call for them to practice and develop their sociolinguistic competence. They have to use language that is appropriate to the situation and to the characters. Students usually find role playing enjoyable, but students who lack self-confidence or have lower proficiency levels may find them intimidating at first. To succeed with role plays:

- *Prepare carefully:* Introduce the activity by describing the situation and making sure that all of the students understand it

- *Set a goal or outcome:* Be sure the students understand what the product of the role play should be, whether a plan, a schedule, a group opinion, or some other product
- *Use role cards:* Give each student a card that describes the person or role to be played. For lower-level students, the cards can include words or expressions that person might use.
- *Brainstorm:* Before you start the role play, have students brainstorm as a class to predict what vocabulary, grammar, and idiomatic expressions they might use.
- *Keep groups small:* Less-confident students will feel more able to participate if they do not have to compete with many voices.
- *Give students time to prepare:* Let them work individually to outline their ideas and the language they will need to express them.
- *Be present as a resource, not a monitor:* Stay in communicative mode to answer students' questions. Do not correct their pronunciation or grammar unless they specifically ask you about it.
- *Allow students to work at their own levels:* Each student has individual language skills, an individual approach to working in groups, and a specific role to play in the activity. Do not expect all students to contribute equally to the discussion, or to use every grammar point you have taught.
- *Do topical follow-up:* Have students report to the class on the outcome of their role plays.
- *Do linguistic follow-up:* After the role play is over, give feedback on grammar or pronunciation problems you have heard. This can wait until another class period when you plan to review pronunciation or grammar anyway.

Discussions, like role plays, succeed when the instructor prepares students first, and then gets out of the way. To succeed with discussions:

- *Prepare the students:* Give them input (both topical information and language forms) so that they will have something to say and the language with which to say it.

– *Offer choices:* Let students suggest the topic for discussion or choose from several options. Discussion does not always have to be about serious issues. Students are likely to be more motivated to participate if the topic is television programmes, plans for a vacation, or news about mutual friends. Weighty topics like how to combat pollution are not as engaging and place heavy demands on students' linguistic competence.

– *Set a goal or outcome:* This can be a group product, such as a letter to the editor, or individual reports on the views of others in the group.

– *Use small groups instead of whole-class discussion:* Large groups can make participation difficult.

– *Keep it short:* Give students a defined period of time, not more than 8-10 minutes, for discussion. Allow them to stop sooner if they run out of things to say.

– *Allow students to participate in their own way:* Not every student will feel comfortable talking about every topic. Do not expect all of them to contribute equally to the conversation.

– Do topical follow-up: Have students report to the class on the results of their discussion.

– Do linguistic follow-up: After the discussion is over, give feedback on grammar or pronunciation problems you have heard. This can wait until another class period when you plan to review pronunciation or grammar anyway.

Through well-prepared communicative output activities such as role plays and discussions, you can encourage students to experiment and innovate with the language, and create a supportive atmosphere that allows them to make mistakes without fear of embarrassment. This will contribute to their self-confidence as speakers and to their motivation to learn more.

5.2.5. Asking and Answering Questions

You may just ask the student to speak, ask him to say something in English. You can even tell him what to say. He may or may not understand the meaning of the utterances he is asked to produce, but he will imitate what you told him to repeat. Another way is to ask the student a question. He will try to answer if he realises that he is being asked to answer a question. For this, he should understand what the question is, and he should have some mastery over the English phonology, grammar, and lexicon necessary to frame an appropriate answer. This is a more difficult task.

Asking and answering questions is an essential part of teaching, learning, and using any language. Asking questions and eliciting answers may be used for various purposes. First of all, asking questions enables the student to practice what he has learned. Secondly, you may ask questions to find whether the student understands the new vocabulary and the structures, and whether he is able to use them appropriately.

5.2.6. Imitation and Repetition

Imitation and repetition are important elementary steps in developing speaking skill in English. Imitation and repetition are interrelated, and yet they are distinct. Imitation helps students to pronounce and produce the English utterance they hear from the teacher as closely as possible to the utterance produced by her. Imitation is not restricted to mere production of the sounds, phrases, and sentences. It includes also the capacity to produce the utterances in the contexts in which the original utterances were produced. On the other hand, repetition refers to the acts of producing the utterances in as close a manner as possible to the original. Repetition leads to automatic reproduction of the utterance, and, in the process, some sort of memorisation of the sound or structure practiced takes place through repetition.

Note, however, that neither imitation nor repetition results in the mastery of any language. Some of the imitation and repetition exercises may be organised in the this manner: Present some simple sentence, phrase, or word and ask students to repeat after you. If you want them to understand and repeat a conversation, say the questions and the answers and have the students repeat the latter, or perhaps both, signalling the meaning in some way. The meaning can be demonstrated with realia (real objects brought into the classroom), pictures, gestures, or translating.

The teacher may use pictures, gestures, pantomime, translation, guessing, and drawing on the board to make the students understand the meaning. It is important that you use only meaningful words, phrases, and sentences for imitation and repetition. The props you use to explain or demonstrate the meaning should enable the student to learn the meaning with ease, along with the pronunciation.

Ask students to repeat the utterance several times. Some learning takes place through repetition, and the student begins to see patterns at different levels. He may form some hypotheses as to the order of occurrence of sounds in a word, words in a phrase, or a sentence. He may begin to distinguish between statements and questions. He may generalise from what he has been exposed to, and form even new sentences based on what he has repeated so far. He may begin to substitute new words in place of the old in the sentences he has repeated and form new sentences.

In the initial phase of learning and teaching English, repetition and imitation serve to make students familiar with the sounds and structures, get the attention and interest of the students, and focus their effort in the learning process. However, if these are stressed continually, or made as the main process of learning, these soon become boring events, and do not contribute to real learning of English. Naturally, the student will commit many errors at first. His pronunciation may not be appropriate, or he may not have reproduced all the elements or units of a word, phrase, or sentence. He will be hampered or guided by the structure and sounds of his language. However, imitation and repetition will help him to practice producing native-like utterances at the sound level.

5.2.7. Substitution

Substitution of a word, phrase, or sentence by another is an elementary method which helps students to produce new utterances and to develop speaking skill. Students repeat the sentence This is a ball several times, and then are given some names of objects such as mat, cat, rat, one after another to substitute in the proper place. In place of this, they may be given that and the students make the substitution and produce a new sentence. That is a mat and so on.

In this way, a sentence frame is practiced first, then suitable slots in the frame are identified for substitution. When substitution is made, a number of new sentences are produced with ease by students. The substitution drill is highly useful for the production of new sentences, it is of limited value (like imitation and repetition) and may not be used as the chief means to develop speaking skill.

Substitution of sounds in minimally different words is a common practice in listening exercises to develop auditory discrimination of sounds. Substitution of one word or phrase by another in the same slot in a frame is a common practice in speaking exercises at the beginners' level. From single word substitution, one may proceed to multiple word substitution in the same slot, without making grammatical changes in the frame: This is a pencil : This is a long pencil.

Consider the following:

- Let's go to the cinema. (theater)
- Let's go to the theater (library).
- Let's go to the library (football).
- Let's play football (hockey).
- Let's play hockey (pizza).
- Let's eat pizza (milk).
- Let's drink milk.

Substitution drills can be made more complex as students learn more structures and words. Combining the substitution drill with processes of addition, deletion and transposition of words/ phrases makes these more complex and challenging to students.

5.2.8. Day-to-day Expressions

Expressions of greeting, gratitude, small talk, introductions and making acquaintance, leave-taking, appreciation, expressions of regret and asking to be excused, etc., are very important communicative acts students need to master. For one thing, such expressions may take on different form and import in English than the ones students are accustomed to in their language and culture. These expressions include, among others, Good morning. How are you?, Fine, Thanks, Hello, How do you do?, and Good-bye. These are learned as they are, with some explanation as to their meaning. Unlike other utterances, these are not analysed into their structural components.

The students may be asked to memorise them and practice using them appropriate to the occasion: Good morning, good afternoon, good evening, good day, good night, etc. You should model their pronunciation and use in appropriate contexts and give students repeated practice so that they can incorporate these in their exchanges with you and other students in the class.

Sentences you teach should be so framed that these are useful and extendable to a variety of real situations. Some cultural information needs to be learned/taught in the use of these expressions. Students may use first names to address one another, but they will be required to use some titles such as Mr. or Mrs. or Dr. when they address adults. They may also use family names to begin with while addressing adults.

Small talk revolves around weather in English. One begins a conversation with another by commenting on weather. Then one introduces himself or herself to the other person. Starting a conversation across the fence, in crowded public places waiting for a game to begin, or in such similar contexts is quite common. This is called phatic communion.

Such phatic communication does not convey a heavy load of information. It functions as icebreakers, to maintain rapport between people, and to signify friendship or lack of enmity. These expressions do vary from culture to culture. Perhaps we, as teachers of English, should learn the phatic communion adopted in the native language of our learners and teach, not only the phatic messages used in native English context, but also incorporate the messages from the culture of the learner as well.

5.2.9. Simple Question-Answer Dialogues

Simple question-answer dialogues around a given context and object/objects is another elementary method to develop speaking skill in students.

There are three types of questions in English: yes/no questions, "or" questions, and WH-questions. Consider these questions which illustrate these types: Do you drink tea? Do you prefer tea or coffee? What do you usually drink? What is this?

Perhaps the easiest question to ask is What is this? Have a number of real objects and pictures of objects with you and ask the question What is this? while pointing to the object. Supply the name of the object and the answer for the question. Following this model, repeat the question and encourage the students to provide the suitable answer.

From this simple process of starting a dialogue, you may proceed to ask more complex questions. Note that the Yes/No questions are also easy to answer. The "Or" questions need more practice to answer.

How do we teach a dialogue? There are three types of drills one could use in the class: choral drill in which the entire class participates in one voice with the teacher modelling the utterance; chain drill in which one student asks the question and another answers, and in this way the entire class participates as a chain; and individual drill in which individual students are pointed out and asked to produce the utterance modelled by the teacher.

We recommend that you start with some form of choral drill, then proceed to chain drill, and finally ask individual students to answer your questions directly (individual drill). The class may be divided into two sections, one section repeating the question and another answering it. If role play is involved, assign roles to the sections. The teacher can assume one of the roles among children. It is always fun when the teacher associates herself with some role and assigns the other roles to students. We can set up puppets, stick figures on the board, pictures, or even live objects for the roles, and the teacher will go behind each of these and produce their utterances as models. The teacher can create pretend situations and give students some model questions to ask these objects. Through dialogue accommodation we modify the dialogues so that the roles and names in the dialogue are made suitable to the participants.

Eliciting long answers helps the student to compose his thoughts in English, search for appropriate words and structures and use them in the appropriate order. This brings out explicitly his grammatical knowledge. Note, however, that in normal conversations long answers are not often expected or given. As their knowledge of and proficiency in using words and structures increase, the teacher can ask her students to talk about real life, about themselves, their friends, things in the world and so on. The teacher can suggest some imaginary situations or the students themselves may assume an imaginary situation and engage themselves in conversation. In such free oral practice, the students may be asked to build the content of a dialogue by giving one sentence each. There will be some initial reluctance on the part of the students, but such reluctance should be overcome.

5.2.10. Eliciting

Eliciting is an important process which teachers must employ to get the class involved in what is going on in the class. For speaking practice eliciting is highly essential. It helps students to focus their attention, to think, and to use what they already know. It helps teachers to assess what the class already knew. Presentation of a lesson with eliciting questions helps students remember words and structures, and gives them practice right then and there when the word is introduced. This may be used even to test the learning level achieved so far within that particular lesson. For example, you may present words for the different parts of the face. Then follow it by eliciting each word by pointing to the feature on your face, asking students what it is called, and then how to spell it. If no one knows the answer for a particular item, give the answer yourself. Use the board to write the words.

In straightforward presentation, the teacher gives the word and points to the part, asks the students to repeat, and then writes the word on the board. In presentation with simple eliciting, the teacher presents the words one by one and points to the parts, asks the students to repeat after her, writes the words on the board, points to the feature and elicits the word for it, and elicits the spelling. Note that, in eliciting, students are actually asked to practice speaking.

You can elicit vocabulary from pictures; you can also elicit sentences and phrases which give the description of what is depicted in the pictures. Ask simple and common questions when you show the pictures to the students. Let the student answer according to each picture. For example, show a picture in which a girl is swimming, and ask the question, What is she doing? Show the picture of a doctor and ask the question, What is this man?

At least two types of questions may be asked using pictures. In Type 1, the questions relate directly to what is seen in the picture. In Type 2, the questions ask students to imagine and interpret the picture beyond what is seen clearly in it.

5.2.11. Guessing

Guessing is important for listening comprehension. Guessing can be used also to develop speaking skill. Through the process of guessing, students are encouraged to see the patterns of usage and to "invent" the correct words and sentences. Students will guess words and sentences that have not yet been taught to them. Through guessing, students work out the rules of deriving new words for themselves.

The teacher writes a few pairs of sentences such as the following on the board:

- He drives buses—He's a bus driver.
- She sells books—She's a book seller.

Based on these examples, students would guess the correct answers for the following.

- Someone who drives trucks (truck driver)
- Someone who owns ships (ship owner)
- Someone who robs banks (bank robber)

You can find lots of such sets of words for eliciting. Egypt-Egyptian, Brazil-Brazilian; Russia-Russian, India-Indian; buy-bought, catch-caught, think-thought; leaf-leaves, loaf-loaves, knife-knives, wife-wives; interesting-more interesting, beautiful-more beautiful; sleep-slept, meet-met, feel-felt; short-shorter, big-bigger.

Mime may be used to encourage students to guess and speak about what is being mimed. The teacher writes an act on a sheet of paper and asks a student to mime what is written on the paper. Other students describe the act as in sentences such as You are changing a light bulb; You are brushing your teeth; You are reading a book.

5.2.12. Directed Dialogues

In Directed Dialogues, the teacher asks a student to make a comment to, or ask a question of, another student. The teacher suggests the content of these remarks: Peter, ask Ann whether she needs some water to drink. Ann, tell Peter that you would like to have a soda.

In such directed dialogues, students must be able to understand what the teacher asks them to do, then identify the appropriate part of the teacher's utterance that would become their response, manipulate the grammatical structure suitably, and then produce the correct response. In this dialogue, the fading of the teacher is more easily done: "Fading involves the withdrawal of the teacher stimulus and participation in an activity as student interest mounts and the activity no longer needs to be sustained by teacher direction. More and more responsibility is passed on to the students".

5.2.13. Show and Tell

In this activity, students are encouraged to bring a favourite toy or object of any kind to class. Let the students bring only those objects which they can handle using the level of competence they have. They show their classmates what they have brought. They also tell them about it: how they got it, where it came from, what is it used for or what it can do, etc. Other students handle the object, try it out, ask questions about it, etc. This provides a good opportunity for self-expression. More often than not, the class would ask WH-questions. The student will also tend to give answers in a form that is possible for him to frame.

5.2.14. Role Play

Role play is perhaps the liveliest form to get the class involved in speaking. Role play brings situations from real life into the classroom. Students imagine and assume roles. They create a pretend situation, and they pretend to be some different persons. Once they assume a role the students are forced to improvise and to produce words and sentences appropriate to the situation as well as to the roles they have assumed. Teachers should select the roles beforehand so that the roles to be assumed are familiar and are within the linguistic competence attained until then by the students.

Roles such as friends, brothers, sisters, parents, teachers, shopkeepers, police officers, characters from the textbook and popular television programmes have been suggested by Doff and others. Everyday life situations such as shopping, holidays, camps, local journeys, fables and folktales, etc., have been found very useful. Interviews are yet another excellent situation for role play.

Students may have difficulty composing their thoughts in English or expressing them coherently, using appropriate grammatical structures and words. Teachers should give prompts wherever necessary, which would encourage students to guess and produce utterances appropriately. Role plays help reduce the common reluctance found among the second language learners in using English because of fear of committing errors in English. Teachers can improve structure practice by encouraging students to give a variety of responses, rather than the usual set responses a situation and a role may demand. The focus of practice should be on producing a text of related sentences suitable for the role and the situation, rather than on the production and practice of single sentences.

Role-play involves several students at once and holds the attention of the class, even as it enables students to be original and produce utterances often on their own. Begin first with the contexts of familiar stories. Go to local contexts including market situations, and then to contexts that may be peculiar to the native English speakers.

References

Brown, and G. Yule, *Teaching the spoken language,* New York: Cambridge University Press, 1983.

Schmidt, R. W., & Frota, S. N., "Developing basic conversational ability in a second language: A case study of an adult learner of Portuguese", In R. R. Day (Ed.), *Talking to learn,* Rowley, MA: Newbury House, 1986.

6

Teaching Pronunciation

English pronunciation involves too many complexities for learners to strive for a complete elimination of accent, but improving pronunciation will boost self esteem, facilitate communication, and possibly lead to a better job or a least more respect in the workplace. Effective communication is of greatest importance, so choose first to work on problems that significantly hinder communication and let the rest go. Remember that your students also need to learn strategies for dealing with misunderstandings, since native pronunciation is for most an unrealistic goal.

6.1. Proper Pronunciation

Pronunciation is a very important component of speaking skill. Without proper pronunciation, which should be somewhat similar to but not necessarily identical to native performance, second or foreign language users of English will not be able to communicate accurately. It is possible to communicate the information without elegant pronunciation. It is also possible to communicate one's intent without elegant pronunciation. However, such communication would be inadequate or could even lead to miscommunication. Moreover, if we allow this to happen all the time and if we do not insist on certain standards of pronunciation, there is a danger that the students would be "led to a permanent plateau of pidgin from which very few emerge".

Remember that pronunciation lends accuracy to the message conveyed. Remember also that if the learner's pronunciation is "very poor", a concept which needs to be clarified and specified in context, he will have great difficulty in communicating orally with native speakers of English. He may have excellent skills in writing and reading, but if his pronunciation is very poor, he will not be seen to be proficient in English. Native speakers of English often tend to be generous towards the second/foreign learners of English. And yet there is always the danger that poor pronunciation may be equated with the lack of knowledge of English.

Pronunciation has been often taught through modelling by the teacher who asks students to listen and imitate her. She corrects the pronunciation, possibly then and there, and asks students to listen and imitate her pronunciation through graded presentation of words, phrases and sentences. Minimal pairs of words such as bit:beat, hit:heat are used to develop correct pronunciation. These may be followed by phrases and sentences for proper sentence melody practice. More often than not, the teacher expects a native-like pronunciation from her students, which the adult students often find impossible to achieve.

The following are the six influencing factors for the of pronunciation:

1. The influence of the learner's native language.
2. The learner's age.
3. The learner's exposure to English – length and intensity of exposure.
4. The learner's innate phonetic ability.
5. The learner's attitude and sense of identity.
6. The learner's motivation and concern for good pronunciation.

The socio-economic class of the learner, whether he comes from a family in which members already know and use some English, and whether there are opportunities available in the community to continue to practice English outside the classroom, may also have an impact upon the level of proficiency attained in the pronunciation of English. The socio-political attitudes towards learning and teaching English which prevail in the nation appear to influence the performance of students in the rural areas.

6.2. Teaching Pronunciation

Teaching pronunciation involves teaching the articulation of consonants, vowels, and diphthongs used in English. These are called segmental sounds. Teaching pronunciation involves teaching also the use of stress and intonation, called suprasegmental. First of all, familiarise yourself with the parts and uses of speech tract. Then, understand the processes involved in the production of the sounds.

6.2.1. Consonant Production

The processes involved in the production of English consonants may be looked at from two angles: manner and places of articulation. Place or point of articulation is the point at which the air from the lungs is either interrupted totally or partly, and is modified in the vocal tract to produce a sound. Scholars identify seven places of articulation in the production of English consonants. These are labial, labiodental, dental, alveolar, palatal, velar, and glottal. Manner of articulation refers to the manner in which the airflow in the vocal tract is modified by the speech organs in the production of a sound. Scholars identify six manners of articulation in the production of English sounds. These are as follows: Stop, Fricative, Affricate, Nasal, Liquid, and Glide.

6.2.2. Vowel Production

The teacher should also have a good knowledge of the processes involved in the production of vowels in English. Vowels pose greater difficulty to the second or foreign language learners of English, especially because of certain complex relations between them, stress, and the production of diphthongs. In the production of a vowel sound there is no interruption whatsoever of the airflow in the speech tract and there is no audible friction either. Four criteria are generally employed in the identification and description of vowels.

1. Lip rounding/unrounding, that is, the kind of opening made at the lips, the degrees of lip rounding or spreading.
2. Tongue height, that is, the extent to which the tongue rises in the direction of the palate.
3. The part of the tongue that is raised: front, center, or back.
4. The position of the soft palate which is raised for the production of oral vowels, and which is closed for the production of nasalised vowels.

It is also important to note whether a vowel is tense or lax and whether a vowel is accompanied by another vowel-like sound which together forms a diphthong. In some cases it is important to note the length of the vowel produced.

6.2.3. Suprasegmentals

The teacher should have a good knowledge of how the suprasegmentals are employed in English. Suprasegmentals are those sounds which are overlaid on segmentals. These do not occur without the segmentals which carry them.

Stress, rhythm, and intonation are the three important elements of the suprasegmental system used in English. Some syllables may be produced with more force or intensity than others. This is called stress. English is a free stress language, unlike French in which the stress always falls on the last syllable of the utterance. In English the stress can be placed on any syllable of the utterance in order to achieve a variety of purposes. The meaning of single words can be changed by shifting the stress. Words which are not ordinarily stressed may be stressed for emphasis.

Remember that recognition (and production) of vowels and stress in English is very difficult for the second or foreign language learners of English. Some rules have been identified to explain why, where, and when the stress falls in a word in English. "Unfortunately, there are no infallible rules for determining which syllable of a word should be stressed. Many times you will need to turn to the dictionary unless you hear the word spoken by someone familiar with it. Certain observations, however, should be of help.

1. The great majority (at least three out of four) of two syllable words are accented on the first syllable: never, breakfast, Monday.
2. Compound expressions:
   - Compound nouns ordinarily have a primary accent on the first component and secondary accent on the second: drugstore, thoroughfare, weatherman.
   - In compound verbs the reverse is true; there is usually secondary accent on the first component and a primary on the second: understand, overlook, outrun.

- In the intensive-reflexive pronouns the stronger accent also falls on the last syllable: myself, yourself.
- Numbers ending in -teen may receive primary stress on either syllable, but it is best for a student learning English as a second language to put it on the last syllable, so as to distinguish clearly between thirty and thirteen, forty and fourteen.

4. A large group of words, which may be used either as nouns or verbs, have a difference in stress to indicate the difference in usage. In such cases, the noun has a primary accent on the first syllable, the verb on the last.
5. In general, when a suffix is added to a word, the new form is stressed on the same syllable as was the basic word: abandon, abandonment; happy, happiness; reason, reasonable. Words ending in -tion, -sion, -ic, -ical, -ity, however, almost always have primary stress on the syllable preceding the ending. The addition of one of these suffixes may, therefore, result in a shift of accent: contribute, contribution; biology, biological; public, publicity."

6.2.4. Focusing on Selected Sounds

Do not teach the sounds of English individually. The sounds should be part of a meaningful word or phrase or sentence. Students generally pick up the sound system by listening to your model or voices on cassette, etc. However, the presentation of sounds in a carefully selected word or phrase or sentence will help you to direct the students' learning process. And this will help you also to monitor their progress. By practising words and phrases which contain the sounds to be learned, students are able to master the production and use of these sounds.

Some suggest that only those sounds that are not common between English and the native language of the learner should be focused upon for special treatment in a pronunciation lesson. Some others suggest that "when an individual begins the study of a foreign language, the new phonemes are often immediately obvious to him, and he, therefore, tends to learn them rather quickly". It may be helpful to make use of a contrastive study of the phonetics of English and the native language of the second or foreign language learner.

Sounds that are used as allophones in the native language may be used as phonemes in English. There may be differences in the number and kinds of phonemes between English and the source language of the learner. Even if all the phonemes of English are found in the source language of the learner, it is possible that their distributional patterns may not match those of the phonemes used in English. It is also possible that the phonemes of English may occur in combinations that are unfamiliar in the source language. English and the native language of the learner may have similar phonemes at different points of articulation.

However, such a contrastive study may or may not be available to you. If you have to prepare such a contrastive study on your own, you will need more skills in linguistics than you may have right now. Making a contrast between English and the native language of the learner should lead you to set up a hierarchy of possible errors in pronunciation. Otherwise mere contrast will be only a futile exercise.

Focus only on those sounds which are causing difficulty to the students. The following steps may be helpful in teaching the difficult sounds:

- Say the sound alone, but this may be avoided wherever possible. Say the sound in a word. Contrast it with other sounds. Write words on the board only when it becomes necessary to make your point clearer. Explain how to make the sound. Have students repeat the sound in chorus. Have individual students repeat the sound.
- Some other steps which you can follow are: use the minimal pairs to practice the sounds (will/well), say a word or phrase with the difficult sound, leaving a blank for the student to fill it in with the known word: A boy and a (girl); First, second and (third); a pigeon is a kind of (bird). You may also make up sentences with words which are difficult for the students to produce, and ask the students to repeat after you and then produce the same on their own.
- Remember that a sound cannot be reproduced by chance. Students must first hear it and recognise. However, we should not spend a lot of time in practising aural discrimination of sounds as a focused activity. Aural

discrimination practice should take only a few minutes of class time.

— Place the new sound in a fixed position in a number of words. Write these words on the board. Model these selected words, giving the same intonation for all words.

— Aural recognition and discrimination is better achieved through minimal pair drills. Contrast two sounds in English in minimal pairs. Contrast two sounds, one in the native language of the leaner and another in English. Often it is helpful to give the approximate equivalent of the English sound in the learner's native language. Emphasize that the similarity is only approximate, wherever some difference is noticeable.

— Model the pairs and then ask students to tell the difference between the pairs of sounds. Same-Different exercise drills are very useful for this purpose. For example, you can give bit/beat/beat and ask which ones are similar and which ones are different. You can give the sentences He bit me/ He beat me and ask the students to show where the difference lies.

6.2.5. Classroom Practice

Pronunciation instruction has been presented in various ways. First there is model of imitation. A second technique for teaching pronunciation is explanation. A third technique is practice. A fourth technique is comparison and contrast.

Face the class, walk around, speak at normal speed, and model the utterance for students to imitate. Produce the sounds in isolation, in isolated words, isolated phrases, and later in sentences. Finally produce them in communicative sentences. Ask the students to imitate your pronunciation. Generally speaking, production of sounds in isolation is for demonstration purposes only. It is always better to produce the sounds in words and phrases which can be easily explained and understood. The new sounds may be given in new words, but not in phrases and sentences which are not understood. Give the meaning for the item which is being drilled. It is always better for the students to drill the words and phrases with their books or sheets open so that they will develop some sensitivity on their own to the correspondence between pronunciation and spelling.

Some of the simple exercises for the pronunciation of sounds are as follows:

- Prepare a list of the sounds used in English. Go through the list and model the same for the students. Ask them to imitate and repeat after you.
- Prepare a list of admissible combination of sounds in English, go through the list, and model the same for the students. Ask them to imitate and repeat after you.
- Prepare a list of very common words, write them as they are usually spelled in English, go through the list, model them for the students, and ask them to imitate and repeat after you.

Then select a few words from the list at random, ask the students to read them, keeping in their auditory memory the model you have provided earlier. In subsequent repetition drills, contrast a newly introduced sound with the one already mastered: pot:putt; lock:luck; rob:rub; duck:dock.

This may be followed by testing drills in which the teacher gives an item and the students recognise the sound in contrast to another. For example, the teacher gives bit and beat as the model. Then she gives words such as hit, heat, leave and live, and asks the students whether the given word resembles in its vowel with hit or heat. Note this kind of testing is more a testing of aural recognition than actual production. However, aural recognition is an important segment of actual production. Production and recognition should go hand in hand.

Always practice in a meaningful context by asking students appropriate questions. In the early part of the pronunciation drill, you may be required to give practice of individual sounds and words without much context. Even here you should explain the meaning of the word in which the sound occurs so that some contextualising will take place.

Once words, phrases and sentences are introduced, context is more easily created. You may ask them to give the names of objects around or in the pictures presented to the students. You may ask the students to give their own names and names of people around them. You may ask questions about their family and friends, what they do, what they did that day, and so on. Words introduced earlier may be used for additional practice by asking students to give the names of objects shown to them or found in the pictures presented to them. This demands recapitulation of the words already introduced.

6.2.6. Teaching Stress and Intonation

As a teacher, you should know what a syllable is. You should be able to identify the syllables in an utterance. Train yourself to identify and count the syllables in words, phrases, and sentences. Remember that most words with two or more syllables have one stressed or strong syllable and one or two unstressed or weak syllables. Stress is not dependent upon the fixed place in the sentence. Stress can occur on any syllable. Generally speaking, only nouns, verbs, adjectives, adverbs, demonstratives and interrogatives are stressed.

Often the vowel in the unstressed syllables is pronounced as / ? / or /I/. Notice the vowel in the beginning of the following words: Asia, apart, attack. All these words have / ? / in the beginning which is unstressed. Notice the first vowel in the word between, and the last vowel in the word wanted. The vowel used is /I/. In the words able, and table, the "a" is pronounced as /eI/ . In vegetable and syllable, it is reduced to / ? /. In the word day, the "ay" is pronounced /eI/ but in the words Monday, and Tuesday, it is often reduced to /I/.

Note also that the vowels in many conjunctions and prepositions such as and, but, at, for, of are normally reduced unless the word is being specially stressed for meaning conveyed. Reducing vowels in this way is a feature of normal spoken English. It is, however, very difficult for the second/foreign language learner to master. You should use and demonstrate reduced vowels in your own speech in the classroom.

When it comes to teaching stress in English, especially to adult learners, it is important that we combine modelling for production with auditory recognition and explanation of possible rules for the placement of the strong stress. For this purpose, you may present several words of polysyllables and ask students to decide which syllable is stressed in each word thus presented. They will mark the primary accent on the vowel in the written word.

English is a stress-timed language. This means that the length of time between stressed syllables is always about the same, and if there are several unstressed syllables they must be said more quickly. He wrote a letter. He wrote a long letter. He wrote a very long letter. In each of these sentences, the unstressed syllables (a, a long, a very long) take about the same amount of time to say. So, "a very long" has to be said more quickly.

Emphasize that this stress timing is a very important feature of spoken English. If students become accustomed to hearing English spoken with a natural rhythm in class, they will find it easier to understand real English when they hear it spoken outside the class. You can use several devices to demonstrate visually where there should be stress and where it should be unstressed. This can be done by using your voice. Say the sentence, exaggerating the difference between stressed and unstressed syllables.

This can be done also by using gesture. Use your arms like a conductor of an orchestra, use a stronger gesture for the stressed syllable. Clapping or tapping on a desk more loudly for the stressed syllables, and less for the unstressed syllables is another technique you can adopt. You can use the black board. You can circle the element in a word which is unstressed, and underline an element that is stressed. You can write the stressed syllable in heavier letters.

Prator, Jr., and Robinett suggest tackling the problem of acquiring a good English speech rhythm under five parts:

1. Giving proper emphasis to stressed syllables, and making these recur rather regularly within a thought group.
2. Weakening unstressed words and syllables, and obscuring the vowels in most of them.
3. Organising words properly into thought groups by means of pauses.
4. Blending the final sound of each word and syllable with the itial sound of the one following within the same thought group.
5. Fitting the entire sentence into a normal intonation pattern.

Remember that content words are usually stressed in English. Content words fall under the following category: Nouns, verbs (with some exceptions), adjectives, adverbs, demonstratives (this, that, these, those) and interrogatives (who, when, why, etc.).

Remember that function words are usually unstressed. Function words which are usually unstressed include the following: Articles (a, an, the), prepositions (to, of, in, etc.), personal pronouns (I, me, he, him, it, etc.), possessive adjectives (my, his, your, etc.), relative pronouns (who, that, which, etc.), common conjunctions (and, but, that, as, if, etc.), one used as a noun-substitute, and the verbs be, have, do, will, would, shall, should, can, could, may, might, and must.

Intonation is speech melody, the way our voice goes up and down as we speak. Intonation is very important in expressing meaning, and especially in showing our feelings, such as surprise, anger, disbelief, gratitude, etc. Intonation patterns are quite complex, and it is better for students to acquire them naturally rather than try to learn them consciously. That is, your modelling and their imitation in an unconscious way is important.

Rising intonation is used in asking yes/no questions, and to express surprise, disbelief, etc. The voice rises sharply on the stressed syllable. Is he your friend? Do you want some tea? "In English, rising intonation is normally used at the end of questions which do not begin with an interrogative word (that is to say, questions which may be answered merely by yes or no)".

Falling intonation is used for normal statements, commands, and for WH-questions. The voice rises slightly earlier in the sentence, and then falls on the key word being stressed. What's your name? Remember that the voice rises slightly earlier in the sentence, and then falls on the key word being stressed. Remember that "the voice often does not rise and fall (suddenly); . . . the change from one tone to another may be gradual and extend over several syllables".

The easiest way for students to practice stress and intonation is by repetition. Prepare sets of sentences with contrasting intonations and give them to the students to practice. You should identify such sentences, wherever possible, from within the lesson.

Give a good model of the sentence. Say it at normal speed, making a clear difference between stressed and unstressed syllables, and using natural intonation. Indicate the stress and intonation clearly, using gestures. Say the sentence in sections, starting with the end of the sentence and gradually working backwards to the beginning. For example, living here/been living here/have you been living here?, etc. Ask groups of students to repeat the whole sentence, then individual students should be asked to repeat the whole sentence. You should watch carefully whether the students pay attention to stress and intonation when they repeat the sentence.

6.2.7. Sound-Spelling Correspondence

Since there is much variation between spelling and pronunciation, it is better to teach these together. When a new sound is learned, give the various spellings of that sound. For example, the learners should recognise that the letter combinations kn, gn, mn, pn, in initial positions have the sound /n/ and that the spelling e has various sounds in different words.

Teach first the common usual spelling of the sound, then follow this with less common spellings, sight words and homophones in that order. Sight words are those words which have a pronunciation different from other words with a similar spelling. For example, look, took, book, shook, good, and wood all form a pattern which is not shared in words such as too, food and mood. These words need to be taught as sight words, as exceptions to the general pattern.

Homophones are words with different spellings which are pronounced the same (two/too/to, night/knight). Homographs are those words with the same or similar spellings with different pronunciation: conduct/conduct, present/present; simply/imply.

Remember that teaching correct and appropriate pronunciation of English to adult learners of English is indeed a very difficult task. Do not expect to eliminate all traces of their native language from their English utterances. The goal is to make them speak English in a manner that their speech, though with the accents of their language, will still be understood fairly well by the native speakers of English.

6.3. Correction of Pronunciation Errors

Correct errors immediately at single word drilling phase. Correct the mistakes by modelling and by asking your students to imitate your pronunciation. In conversational exchanges, correct errors only on particular teaching points. Correct those items which interfere with comprehensibility, and overlook other mistakes. Judge content and form separately.

Correct carefully without reducing motivation and self-image of the adult learners. There are three approaches to error correction practiced by teachers.

1. "I never let my students make mistakes. If they say anything wrong, I stop them and make them say it correctly. I don't want them to learn bad English from each other." This approach focuses more on errors of students than on what they do correctly. This approach hampers developing fluency in English, for committing mistakes is an integral part of any learning activity. Currently it is agreed that the errors committed by the students should be considered as an indication of what we still need to teach.
2. "I correct students sometimes, but not all the time. If we're practising one particular language point, then I insist that they say it correctly. But if we're doing a freer activity then I try not to correct too much. If I do correct, I try to do it in an encouraging way."
3. "I try to correct errors as little as possible. I want my students to express themselves in English without worrying too much about making mistakes. Sometimes I notice points that everyone gets wrong, and deal with them later – but I never interrupt students to correct them."

Presently, "most teachers would agree . . . that we need to correct some errors, to help students learn the correct forms of the language . . . But this does not mean that we have to correct students all the time – if we do, it might make them unwilling or unable to say anything at all".

Praise students for correct answers, and even for partly correct answers; in this way, they will feel they are making progress. Avoid humiliating students or making them feel that making a mistake is 'bad'. Correct errors quickly; if too much time is spent over correcting errors, it gives them too much importance and holds up the lesson".

REFERENCES

Avery, P.- Ehrlich, S. (Eds.), *The Teaching of Pronunciation: An Introduction for Teachers of English as a Second Language*, Oxford: Oxford University Press, 1987.

Brown, A. (Ed.), *Teaching English Pronunciation*, A Book of Readings, London: Routledge, 1991.

_______________, *Approaches to Pronunciation Teaching*, London: Macmillan, 1992.

Celce-Murcia, M, Brinton, D, Goodwin, J., *Teaching pronunciation: A reference for teachers of English to speakers of other languages*, New York: Cambridge University Press, 1996.

Dalton, C, Seidlhofer, B., *Pronunciation*, Oxford: Oxford University Press, 1994.

Fraser, H., *Teaching Pronunciation: A handbook for teachers and trainers*, Sydney: TAFE Access Division (funded by the Adult Literacy Project through the Commonwealth of Australia Department of Education Training and Youth Affairs), 2001.

Haycraft, B., *The Teaching of Pronunciation: A Classroom guide*, London: Longman, 1971.

Kenworthy, J., *Teaching English Pronunciation*, London: Longman, 1987.

Laroy, C., *Pronunciation*, Oxford: Oxford University Press, 1995.

Scarcella, R.C.- Oxford, R.L., "Second language pronunciation: state of the art in instruction", *System 22*, 1994.

Setter, J.- Jenkins, J., "Pronunciation", *Language Teaching*, 2005.

7

Teaching Listening

Listening in English is attending to and interpreting oral English. Listening is necessary to develop the speaking skill. The student listens to oral speech in English, then separates into segments the stretch of utterances he hears, groups them into words, phrases, and sentences, and, finally, he understands the message these carry. Listening prepares the students to understand the speech of the native speakers of English as they speak naturally in a normal speed and normal manner.

There are three approaches to listening: interactive (listening to a message and doing something as a consequence) and one-way communication or non-interactive (just listening and retaining the message, in activities such as conversations overheard, public address announcements, recorded messages, etc.) and self-talk. Listening to radio and watching TV and films, public performances, lectures, religious services, etc., generally reflect non-interactive listening. Responding to the commands given reflects interactive listening, which, in fact, is equally widespread in communicative situations. Self-talk is also an important process by which internal thinking and reasoning is carried out.

In the classroom, students listen in order to repeat and to understand. In listening to repeat, students imitate and memorise linguistic items such as words, idioms, and sentence patterns. This is an important beginning task and focus of listening exercises. However, it is listening to understand that is real listening in its own right. Students listen to understand as part of using English for communication purposes. In listening to understand, students may be involved in the question-oriented response model of learning or in the task-oriented model of learning. In the question-oriented response model, students may be asked to listen to a sentence, a dialogue, a conversation, a passage, or a lecture and asked to answer questions which may be presented in the form of true/false statements, multiple choice questions, fill in blank, or short answers. In the task-oriented response model, students may be asked to listen to a passage and accomplish the task described in the passage through interaction with others or by themselves.

Most students have difficulty with listening skills, even when listening to their native language. Among other factors, because of the phenomenon of stress, most learners of English have difficulty in mastering the correct placement of the primary and other stresses in English. As a consequence, listening proficiency in English is to be cultivated with great care.

7.1. Goals and Techniques for Teaching Listening

Instructors want to produce students who, even if they do not have complete control of the grammar or an extensive lexicon, can fend for themselves in communication situations. In the case of listening, this means producing students who can use listening strategies to maximise their comprehension of aural input, identify relevant and non-relevant information, and tolerate less than word-by-word comprehension.

To accomplish this goal, instructors focus on the process of listening rather than on its product.

- They develop students' awareness of the listening process and listening strategies by asking students to think and talk about how they listen in their native language.
- They allow students to practice the full repertoire of listening strategies by using authentic listening tasks.
- They behave as authentic listeners by responding to student communication as a listener rather than as a teacher.
- When working with listening tasks in class, they show students the strategies that will work best for the listening purpose and the type of text. They explain how and why students should use the strategies.
- They have students practice listening strategies in class and ask them to practice outside of class in their listening

assignments. They encourage students to be conscious of what they're doing while they complete listening tape assignments.

- They encourage students to evaluate their comprehension and their strategy use immediately after completing an assignment. They build comprehension checks into in-class and out-of-class listening assignments, and periodically review how and when to use particular strategies.
- They encourage the development of listening skills and the use of listening strategies by using the target language to conduct classroom business: making announcements, assigning homework, describing the content and format of tests.
- They do not assume that students will transfer strategy use from one task to another. They explicitly mention how a particular strategy can be used in a different type of listening task or with another skill.

By raising students' awareness of listening as a skill that requires active engagement, and by explicitly teaching listening strategies, instructors help their students develop both the ability and the confidence to handle communication situations they may encounter beyond the classroom. In this way they give their students the foundation for communicative competence in the new language.

7.2. Developing Listening Skills

Language learning depends on listening. Listening provides the aural input that serves as the basis for language acquisition and enables learners to interact in spoken communication. Effective language instructors show students how they can adjust their listening behaviour to deal with a variety of situations, types of input, and listening purposes. They help students develop a set of listening strategies and match appropriate strategies to each listening situation.

7.2.1. Listening Strategies

Listening strategies are techniques or activities that contribute directly to the comprehension and recall of listening input.

Listening strategies can be classified by how the listener processes the input.

Top-down strategies are listener based; the listener taps into background knowledge of the topic, the situation or context, the type of text, and the language. This background knowledge activates a set of expectations that help the listener to interpret what is heard and anticipate what will come next. Top-down strategies include:

- listening for the main idea
- predicting
- drawing inferences
- summarising

Bottom-up strategies are text based; the listener relies on the language in the message, that is, the combination of sounds, words, and grammar that creates meaning. Bottom-up strategies include:

- listening for specific details
- recognising cognates
- recognising word-order patterns

Strategic listeners also use *metacognitive strategies* to plan, monitor, and evaluate their listening.

- They plan by deciding which listening strategies will serve best in a particular situation.
- They monitor their comprehension and the effectiveness of the selected strategies.
- They evaluate by determining whether they have achieved their listening comprehension goals and whether the combination of listening strategies selected was an effective one.

7.2.2. Developing Listening Activities

As you design listening tasks, keep in mind that complete recall of all the information in an aural text is an unrealistic expectation to which even native speakers are not usually held. Listening exercises that are meant to train should be success-oriented and build up students' confidence in their listening ability.

7.2.3. Contextualised Listening

Contextualised listening activities approximate real-life tasks and give the listener an idea of the type of information to expect and what to do with it in advance of the actual listening. A beginning level task would be locating places on a map (one way) or exchanging name and address information (two way). At an intermediate level students could follow directions for assembling something (one way) or work in pairs to create a story to tell to the rest of the class (two way).

Each activity should have as its goal the improvement of one or more specific listening skills. A listening activity may have more than one goal or outcome, but be careful not to overburden the attention of beginning or intermediate listeners. Recognising the goal(s) of listening comprehension in each listening situation will help students select appropriate listening strategies.

- *Identification:* Recognising or discriminating specific aspects of the message, such as sounds, categories of words, morphological distinctions
- *Orientation:* Determining the major facts about a message, such as topic, text type, setting
- *Main idea comprehension:* Identifying the higher-order ideas
- *Detail comprehension:* Identifying supporting details
- *Replication:* Reproducing the message orally or in writing

7.2.4. Difficulty of the listening text

The factors listed below can help you judge the relative ease or difficulty of a listening text for a particular purpose and a particular group of students.

- How is the information organised? Does the story line, narrative, or instruction conform to familiar expectations? Texts in which the events are presented in natural chronological order, which have an informative title, and which present the information following an obvious organisation (main ideas first, details and examples second) are easier to follow.
- How familiar are the students with the topic? Remember that misapplication of background knowledge due to

cultural differences can create major comprehension difficulties.

- Does the text contain redundancy? At the lower levels of proficiency, listeners may find short, simple messages easier to process, but students with higher proficiency benefit from the natural redundancy of the language.
- Does the text involve multiple individuals and objects? Are they clearly differentiated? It is easier to understand a text with a doctor and a patient than one with two doctors, and it is even easier if they are of the opposite sex. In other words, the more marked the differences, the easier the comprehension.
- Does the text offer visual support to aid in the interpretation of what the listeners hear? Visual aids such as maps, diagrams, pictures, or the images in a video help contextualise the listening input and provide clues to meaning.

Use pre-listening activities to prepare students for what they are going to hear or view.

The activities chosen during pre-listening may serve as preparation for listening in several ways. During pre-listening the teacher may

- assess students' background knowledge of the topic and linguistic content of the text
- provide students with the background knowledge necessary for their comprehension of the listening passage or activate the existing knowledge that the students possess
- clarify any cultural information which may be necessary to comprehend the passage
- make students aware of the type of text they will be listening to, the role they will play, and the purpose(s) for which they will be listening
- provide opportunities for group or collaborative work and for background reading or class discussion activities

While-listening activities relate directly to the text, and students do them do during or immediately after the time they are listening. Keep these points in mind when planning while-listening activities:

- If students are to complete a written task during or immediately after listening, allow them to read through it before listening. Students need to devote all their attention to the listening task. Be sure they understand the instructions for the written task before listening begins so that they are not distracted by the need to figure out what to do.
- Keep writing to a minimum during listening. Remember that the primary goal is comprehension, not production. Having to write while listening may distract students from this primary goal. If a written response is to be given after listening, the task can be more demanding.
- Organise activities so that they guide listeners through the text. Combine global activities such as getting the main idea, topic, and setting with selective listening activities that focus on details of content and form.
- Use questions to focus students' attention on the elements of the text crucial to comprehension of the whole. Before the listening activity begins, have students review questions they will answer orally or in writing after listening. Listening for the answers will help students recognise the crucial parts of the message.
- Use predicting to encourage students to monitor their comprehension as they listen. Do a predicting activity before listening, and remind students to review what they are hearing to see if it makes sense in the context of their prior knowledge and what they already know of the topic or events of the passage.

Give immediate feedback whenever possible. Encourage students to examine how or why their responses were incorrect.

7.2.5. Textbook Listening Activities

The greatest challenges with textbook tape programmes are integrating the listening experiences into classroom instruction and keeping up student interest and motivation. These challenges arise from the fact that most textbook listening programmes emphasise product (right or wrong answer) over process (how to get meaning from the selection) and from the fact that the listening activities are usually carried out as an add-on, away from the classroom.

You can use the guidelines for developing listening activities given here as starting points for evaluating and adapting textbook listening programmes. At the beginning of the teaching term, orient students to the tape programme by completing the exercises in class and discussing the different strategies they use to answer the questions. It is a good idea to periodically complete some of the lab exercises in class to maintain the link to the regular instructional programme and to check on the effectiveness of the exercises themselves.

Students can use this outline for both in-class and out-of-class listening/viewing activities. Model and practice the use of the outline at least once in class before you ask students to use it independently.

1. Plan for listening/viewing
   - Review the vocabulary list, if you have one
   - Review the worksheet, if you have one
   - Review any information you have about the content of the tape/video
2. Preview the tape/video
   - (tape) Use fast forward to play segments of the tape; (video) view the video without sound
   - Identify the kind of programme (news, documentary, interview, drama)
   - Make a list of predictions about the content
   - Decide how to divide the tape/video into sections for intensive listening/viewing
3. Listen/view intensively section by section. For each section:
   - Jot down key words you understand
   - Answer the worksheet questions pertaining to the section

- If you don't have a worksheet, write a short summary of the section

4. Monitor your comprehension
   - Does it fit with the predictions you made?
   - Does your summary for each section make sense in relation to the other sections?
5. Evaluate your listening comprehension progress

7.2.6. Teaching Listening Comprehension

The listening skill is the most neglected one, both in first and second language teaching. Teachers tend to focus on the rudimentary elements of listening briefly, and pass over to other aspects of language teaching. Discrimination of sounds and intonations often form the major part of listening practice in the classroom. Listening for content is often assumed. In reality, the listening skill is fundamental to the entire process of mastering and using a language, whether first or second or foreign.

Listening is like painting, like colour, in day to day environment. You don't notice, but it is always there in every linguistic activity. Listening is important for casual chats, face to face encounters, telephone messages, for enjoyment of radio and television programmes, formal lectures, and many other activities. In the past, listening was labelled as a passive skill, along with reading. No doubt, it is a receptive skill like reading. Speaking and writing were considered to be productive skills, but also active skills. While this categorisation is somewhat justifiable because the focus of listening is on reception of information, listening itself cannot be fully and correctly characterised only as a passive skill.

There is a need for an active involvement of the self for the efficient performance of listening. The listener is often forced into guessing an approximation to what the speaker is communicating. The listener expects and anticipates what may be the form and content of the immediate message being delivered. He actively avoids the redundancies in the process of listening, focuses himself on the relevant, interesting and/or crucial points, and engages himself in some critical analysis of content. Listening becomes the stepping stone for action. In view of all these and other activities that are involved in listening, we should consider listening as an active skill demanding active participation of the listener.

Listening is an integral part of any type of language performance. Teachers should enable the students to listen to native speakers' speech from the beginning. The students are always required to listen to the teacher's instructions and questions, and answer them. They may listen to conversations between a student and the teacher and understand what is going on. They may like to participate in a discussion between students and understand what is being discussed. They may like to listen and enjoy the story told by the teacher, and answer questions raised by the teacher. They may listen to simple questions eliciting information about them and their families and understand what the speaker wants to know from them. They may enjoy the jokes told both in the class and outside.

Outside the classroom, the students have many needs which they can meet only by listening to the speech around them and by expressing what they need. They need to understand the native speakers of English they come across in their day to day life, if they are studying and/or working in an English speaking country. Where there is no opportunity for them to come across native English speakers, they will need to listen and comprehend the native English used in the movies and TV programmes.

7.2.6.1. Principles of Teaching Listening Comprehension

In the early stages of listening, the students may have to be taught and exposed to discrimination of sounds used in English in isolation as well as in combination, not simply as sounds in themselves in isolation, but as units of meaningful words. The goals of teaching listening comprehension to a beginning student of English are different from those when teaching English to an advanced student. The advanced student has already mastered the discrimination of sounds and their combinations as well as various other aspects of phrases and sentences such as the significance of pauses between words and phrases, sentence intonation, etc. Therefore, he is geared towards following the flow of content of the message in such a way that he is not conscious of the mechanics or the processes of listening.

In essence, listening is not mere recognition of linguistic units and their meanings. It comprises an ability to predict information based on linguistic context, and the situation and topic of the message conveyed by the linguistic code, as well as the expectations about the world. Listening helps also to understand and act according to the emotional state of the speaker. First of all, you should be clear about your goals in teaching a lesson for listening comprehension. These goals must be made explicit and explained to the students so that the learning process becomes meaningful to them. Secondly, you should plan for a careful step by step progression in the material and, in teaching the same in the class. You should give direction to the students as to what they should listen for, where to listen, when to listen, and how to listen. Thirdly, you must insist on active overt student participation. They should provide some written or physical response. Listening is done silently, but needs to be demonstrated through some other overt manifestation.

Organise your lesson in such a way that there is a need for the students to develop concentration while listening and for remembering (and reproducing) what they have listened to. This does not mean that you should clutter your lesson with facts, figures and details. Even with very little details, we may be able to create a need to listen intently, if the material is based on a communicative need.

It is important that students develop consciously their memory span while listening to a message. Their auditory memory span must be strengthened and expanded in progressive steps in English. While personality factors play a very important role in deciding how successful a listener a student could become, the learners need to have some minimal competence in listening to the speech of the native speakers. In due course they should be able to listen and remember relatively lengthy sentences and phrases.

In natural contexts, no one deliberately speaks in very long sentences. Often we tend to use certain sentence patterns more frequently than others. The number of adjectives in a noun phrase often is limited and these often follow a certain order. The teachers can take advantage of such structural information and build their classroom listening practice around these.

Listening, thinking, and remembering go together. They are not separate acts. The teacher should organise her lesson and its presentation and teaching in the class in such a way that listening, thinking, and remembering are all integrated in listening comprehension. Neither you nor your students should think that listening comprehension exercises are miniature tests. These generally come in the form of questions to be answered, action to be performed, or objects to be identified, etc. Because this format demands response in the form in which tests are generally prepared and presented, we tend to treat the exercise as a test. Consider listening comprehension only as practice and look for progress in student performance.

Task-orientation materials focus on performance based on what is presented as listening material. There are at least six types of task-oriented use: Listening and performing actions; Listening and performing operations (listening and constructing a figure, drawing a map, etc.), Listening and solving problems (riddles, numerical, spatial or chronological problems), Listening and transcribing (taking telephone messages, writing notes), Listening and summarising information. Interactive listening and negotiating meaning through questioning and answering routines. Note that every one of these items can be used as exercise types.

At the classroom techniques for developing listening under seven major heads:

Developing cognitive strategies (listening for the main idea, listening for details, and predicting), Developing listening with other skills (listening and speaking, listening and pronunciation, and listening and vocabulary), Listening to authentic material (such as weather reports, television daytime dramas, News, Discussions, Advertisements, etc.), Using technology (Phone mail, recording messages, etc.), Listening for academic purposes, and Listening for fun.

A generally followed format of listening comprehension lessons includes the following:

1. Select the teaching point for the listening comprehension lesson.

2. Introduce the topic before the class begins to listen to the passage. In this manner the teacher brings the students' attention to focus on the material to be listened to.
3. Give one or two guiding questions before students begin to listen to the passage.
4. Divide the listening into stages, such as listening for the main idea only at the first instance, then answering some guiding questions.
5. Divide the passage into several sections and check comprehension after each section.
6. Students listen to the passage and complete the set task.
7. Presentation of feed back on the performance of the students.
8. You may read the passage once again so that your students may follow the passage more fully.

More often than not, a well graded listening comprehension lesson selects the teaching points (that is, the material to be listened to) from all the components of language. Listening does not focus only upon the sounds in isolation or in combination, even though such training to discriminate between various sounds of the English language may be necessary at the beginning level. It may begin with the discrimination of sounds and may proceed to the discriminations of sounds in combination, words, phrases, clauses and sentences. It focuses on the discrimination of various intonation patterns, and grammatical structures. However, the ultimate goal of listening is to listen for information.

There are several kinds of listening comprehension exercises.

1. A rudimentary but important form of listening comprehension exercise is the Use of the terms in English for class management. The teacher frequently uses instructions such as Everybody sit down; Listen carefully; Answer; Again; and Repeat. When these are uttered with appropriate gestures, the students begin to understand them very soon.
2. While use of the class management terms is continued, introduce as part of your lesson Physical Response Activities. Commands would be given by the teacher and

the students would give appropriate physical responses: Stand up; Walk to the window; Open the Window. You as a teacher of English as a foreign/second language can demonstrate the act intended to be carried out by the students initially.

3. Limited Verbal Response Activities. The response in these exercises is limited to yes/no, true/false, simple answers to WH-questions, usually answers that consist of one word. Do not emphasise production of complete answers.
4. Sound Discrimination Exercises. In English, consonant discrimination is more easily learned than vowel discrimiration. And vowel discrimination is more easily learned than stress discrimination and production. Teaching of English stress is important in contrastive contexts.
5. There are many one-syllable words such as and, to, for, than, the, was, etc., which, when buried in sentences, are unstressed and, as a consequence, cause listening problems to the second language learners of English. This problem is not generally recognised in the classroom, but in actual conditions of language use it hinders listening. One way to overcome this problem is to teach some nursery rhymes which abound in unstressed syllables and words: One for the money, Two for the show, Three to get ready, And four to go. Note that all the underlined items are unstressed words.

   Since unstressed syllables and words cause listening problems and consequent misunderstanding of what is being listened to, you should continually provide your students with exercises for listening to the unstressed syllables and words. Some of the following exercises may be used: Check every time you hear and. Check every time you hear to. Check every time you hear for, and similar exercises for the unstressed items. Another complex exercise would be to ask the students how many times the word for (etc.) occurs in the text?
6. Often we tend to focus less attention upon teaching the segmental sounds and their combinations in English. However, mastering some of the segmental sounds and

their combinations could pose some difficulty to second language learners.

7. There are also difficulties faced by learners in mastering combinations of segmental sounds. Often, the clusters of sounds in the word's initial position may pose some difficulty. For example, many Punjabi speakers have difficulty in mastering the pronunciation of the clusters such as st-, sl-, sp-and sk-. Once again a contrastive minimal pair drill in which the contrast between the occurrence of single sounds and their combinations could be designed: sick vs. stick. Note that we are not talking about producing the sequences of sounds, but about listening to discriminate the sequences of sounds.

   It would be highly useful if you had some idea of the nature of the phonology of the source language of your students. This would give you some insights into the difficulties posed by your class, and you could come up with some concrete illustrations as to why they have difficulty in listening to particular speech sounds and/or their combinations.

8. While certain intonation patterns (sentence melody), based upon the universality of emotions in some sense, could be easily recognised by the students, others, which carry communicative nuances such as sarcasm, cynicism, wonder, doubt, etc., will be hard to follow. Hence there is a need to teach your class a variety of intonations the native speakers of English generally use in their day to day language.

9. The student is required not only to comprehend native English spoken to him, but also to comprehend it with a speed that somewhat matches the speed of comprehension in a natural language situation in English. Accordingly, your listening exercise should have some room for the development of "listening speed." An important step towards this is to ask the learners to make intelligent guesses about the meaning based on the context of other words in the utterances.

In short, listening is an important part of the competence of a successful learner of English. Listening can be dealt with in isolation, through exercises which focus on listening aspects only. However, even as we focus on it as an independent skill in the learning of English, it is important for us to integrate listening with speaking through all the lessons. This may be better accomplished if we deliberately include some listening exercises in every lesson we teach.

References

Byrnes, H., "The role of listening comprehension: A theoretical base", *Foreign Language Annals,* 1984.

Lund, R.J., "A taxonomy for teaching second language listening", *Foreign Language Annals,* 1990.

Mendelsohn, D.J., & Rubin, J., *A guide for the teaching of second language listening,* San Diego, CA: Dominie Press, 1995.

Morley, J., "Listening comprehension in second/foreign language instruction", In M. Celce-Murcia (Ed.), *Teaching English as a second or foreign language,* Boston, MA: Heinle & Heinle, 1991.

Nunan, D., & Miller, L.(Eds.), *New ways in teaching listening,* Alexandria, VA: TESOL, 1995.

Omaggio-Hadley, A., *Teaching language in context (2nd ed.),* Boston, MA: Heinle & Heinle, 1993.

Richards, J.C., "Listening comprehension: Approach, design, procedure", *TESOL Quarterly,* 1983.

Rost, M., *Listening in language learning,* London: Longman, 1990.

Rubin, J., "The contribution of video to the development of competence in listening", In D.J. Mendelsohn & J. Rubin (Eds.), *A guide for the teaching of second language listening,* San Diego, CA: Dominie Press, 1995.

Underwood, M., *Teaching listening,* London: Longman, 1989.

8

Teaching English Writing Skills

Writing and reading are both vital aspects of literacy, they each require their own dedicated instruction. What improves reading does not always improve writing. In the school setting, writing plays two distinct but complementary roles. First, it is a skill that draws on the use of strategies (such as planning, evaluating, and revising text) to accomplish a variety of goals, such as writing a report or expressing an opinion with the support of evidence. Second, writing is a means of extending and deepening students' knowledge; it acts as a tool for learning subject matter.

In an ideal world, teachers would be able to incorporate all of the 11 key elements in their everyday writing curricula, but the list may also be used to construct a unique blend of elements suited to specific student needs. The elements should not be seen as isolated but rather as interlinked. For instance, it is difficult to implement the process writing approach without having peers work together or use prewriting supports. A mixture of these elements is likely to generate the biggest return. It remains to be seen what that optimal mix is, and it may be different for different subpopulations of students. However, it is important to stress that these 11 elements are not meant to constitute a curriculum.

The instructional elements are ordered according to their average effect. Therefore, elements with larger effect sizes are presented before those with smaller effect sizes. However, many of the effect sizes differ only minimally, so readers should be cautious in interpreting the differences in effect strength.

8.1. Writing Instruction

Writing quality is defined here in terms of coherently organised essays containing well-developed and pertinent ideas, supporting examples, and appropriate detail. Writing quality was included as the primary outcome, or one of several primary outcomes, in all previous meta-analyses on procedures for teaching writing. Writing quality served as the sole outcome measure because the authors were interested in identifying treatments that had a broad impact on writing performance. The only exceptions involved studies examining the teaching of summarisation, in which completeness and accuracy of summaries were assessed, and writing-to-learn studies, in which content learning was the outcome measure.

8.1.1. Elements of Writing Instruction

8.1.1.1. Writing Strategies

Teaching adolescents strategies for planning, revising, and editing their compositions has shown a dramatic effect on the quality of students' writing. Strategy instruction involves explicitly and systematically teaching steps necessary for planning, revising, and/or editing text. The ultimate goal is to teach students to use these strategies independently. Strategy instruction may involve teaching more generic processes, such as brainstorming or collaboration for peer revising. In other instances, it involves teaching strategies for accomplishing specific types of writing tasks, such as writing a story or a persuasive essay. Whether generic or highly focused, explicitly teaching adolescents strategies for planning, revising, and/or editing has a strong impact on the quality of their writing. Writing strategy instruction has been found especially effective for adolescents who have difficulty writing, but it is also a powerful technique for adolescents in general.

Self-Regulated Strategy Development (SRSD) is a particularly effective approach for teaching writing strategies. The average weighted effect size for SRSD studies was larger than for non-SRSD studies. SRSD is characterised by explicit instruction of writing strategies and self-regulation procedures (e.g., self-assessment and goal setting), as well as individualised instruction and criterion-based learning. Although SRSD had stronger effects than most other strategy approaches, the meta-analysis indicates moderate to strong effects of writing strategy instruction in general.

8.1.1.2. Summarisation

Writing instruction often involves explicitly and systematically teaching students how to summarise texts. The summarisation approaches studied ranged from explicitly teaching summarisation strategies to enhancing summarisation by progressively "fading" models of a good summary. In fact, students can learn to write better summaries from either a rule-governed or a more intuitive approach. Overall, teaching adolescents to summarise text had a consistent, strong, positive effect on their ability to write good summaries.

8.1.1.3. Collaborative Writing

Collaborative writing involves developing instructional arrangements whereby adolescents work together to plan, draft, revise, and edit their compositions. It shows a strong impact on improving the quality of students' writing. Studies of this approach compared its effectiveness with that of having students compose independently. The effect sizes for all studies were positive and large. Collectively, these investigations show that collaborative arrangements in which students help each other with one or more aspects of their writing have a strong positive impact on quality. It was not possible to draw separate conclusions for low-achieving writers, as only two studies involved these students specifically.

8.1.1.4. Specific Product Goals

Setting product goals involves assigning students specific, reachable goals for the writing they are to complete. It includes identifying the purpose of the assignment (e.g., to persuade) as well as characteristics of the final product. Specific goals in the studies reviewed included (a) adding more ideas to a paper when revising, or establishing a goal to write a specific kind of paper and (b) assigning goals for specific structural elements in a composition. Compared with instances in which students were simply given a general overall goal, these relatively simple procedures resulted in a positive effect size, and the average effect was strong. It was possible to obtain effect sizes specifically for low-achieving writers in three of the five product goal studies. The average effect for these students was similarly strong, providing some tentative evidence that, interpreted cautiously (because of the small sample), indicates that setting product goals is effective with adolescents who are weaker writers. Overall, assigning students goals for their written product had a strong impact on writing quality.

8.1.1.5. Word Processing

The use of word-processing equipment can be particularly helpful for low-achieving writers. In this type of instruction, students might work collaboratively on writing assignments using personal laptop computers, or they might learn to word-process a composition under teacher guidance. Typing text on the computer with word-processing software produces a neat and legible script. It allows the writer to add, delete, and move text easily. Word-processing software, especially in more recent studies, includes spell checkers as well.

Compared with composing by hand, the effect of word-processing instruction in most of the studies reviewed was positive, suggesting that word processing has a consistently positive impact on writing quality. The average effect on writing quality was moderate for students in general, but for low-achieving writers it was larger. Thus, word processing appears to be an effective instructional support for students in grades 4 to 12 and may be especially effective in enhancing the quality of text produced by low-achieving writers.

8.1.1.6. Sentence Combining

Sentence combining involves teaching students to construct more complex and sophisticated sentences through exercises in which two or more basic sentences are combined into a single sentence. Teaching adolescents how to write increasingly complex sentences in this way enhances the quality of their writing. Studies establishing the effectiveness of sentence combining primarily compared it with more traditional grammar instruction. The effect sizes for all studies were consistently positive and moderate in strength.

8.1.1.7. Pre-writing

Pre-writing engages students in activities designed to help them generate or organise ideas for their composition. Engaging adolescents in such activities before they write a first draft improves the quality of their writing. Pre-writing activities include gathering possible information for a paper through reading or developing a visual representation of their ideas before sitting down to write. For example, some common pre-writing activities include encouraging group and individual planning before writing, organising pre-writing ideas, prompting students to plan after providing a brief demonstration of how to do so, or assigning reading material pertinent to a topic and then encouraging students to plan their work in advance. It was not possible to draw separate conclusions for low-achieving writers, as all of the pre-writing studies involved students across the full range of ability in regular classrooms. Collectively, these investigations show that pre-writing activities have a positive and small to moderate impact on the quality of students' writing.

8.1.1.8. Inquiry Activities

Inquiry means engaging students in activities that help them develop ideas and content for a particular writing task by analysing immediate, concrete data (comparing and contrasting cases or collecting and evaluating evidence). Involving adolescents in writing activities designed to sharpen their inquiry skills improves the quality of their writing. Effective inquiry activities in writing are characterised by a clearly specified goal (e.g., describe the actions of people), analysis of concrete and immediate data (observe one or more peers during specific activities), use of specific strategies to conduct the analysis (retrospectively ask the person being observed the reason for a particular action), and applying what was learned (assign the writing of a story incorporating insights from the inquiry process).

8.1.1.9. Process Writing Approach

The process writing approach involves a number of interwoven activities, including creating extended opportunities for writing; emphasising writing for real audiences; encouraging cycles of planning, translating, and reviewing; stressing personal responsibility and ownership of writing projects; facilitating high levels of student interactions; developing supportive writing environments; encouraging self-reflection and evaluation; and offering personalised individual assistance, brief instructional lessons to meet students' individual needs, and, in some instances, more extended and systematic instruction. The overall effect of the process writing approach was small to moderate, but significant.

8.1.1.10. Study of Models

The study of models provides adolescents with good models for each type of writing that is the focus of instruction. Students are encouraged to analyse these examples and to emulate the critical elements, patterns, and forms embodied in the models in their own writing.The effects for all six studies reviewed were positive, though small. It was not possible to draw separate conclusions for low-achieving writers, as none of the studies specifically addressed this population.

8.1.1.11. Writing for Content Area Learning

Writing has been shown to be an effective tool for enhancing students' learning of content material. Although the impact of writing activity on content learning is small, it is consistent enough to predict some enhancement in learning as a result of writing-to-learn activities. About 75% of the writing-to-learn studies analysed had positive effects. The average effect was small but significant.

8.1.2. Grammar Instruction

Grammar instruction for students across the full range of ability, but surprisingly, this effect was negative. This negative effect was small, but it was statistically significant, indicating that traditional grammar instruction is unlikely to help improve the quality of students' writing. Studies specifically examining the impact of grammar instruction with low-achieving writers also yielded negative results. Such findings raise serious questions about some educators' enthusiasm for traditional grammar instruction as a focus of writing instruction for adolescents. However, other instructional methods, such as sentence combining, provide an effective alternative to traditional grammar instruction, as this approach improves students' writing quality while at the same time enhancing syntactic skills.

Although currently eclipsed by reading instruction, teaching students to write played a central role in education in many historical periods, from ancient Greek times through the 19th century. Indeed, writing well was once a central goal of education in both Europe and the United States. However, what is valued in writing, and thus the focus of writing instruction, has changed over the years.

8.1.3. Aims of Writing Instruction

Modern writing instruction in the United States recognises that students need to write clearly and for a wide variety of real-life purposes. Thus, *flexibility* is now perhaps the most prized goal of writing instruction because the fully proficient writer can adapt to different contexts, formats, and purposes for writing.

Most contexts of life (school, the workplace, and the community) call for writing skills, and each context makes overlapping but not identical demands. Proficient writers can adapt their writing to its context. Writing is also produced in different formats, such as sentences, lists, outlines, paragraphs, essays, letters, and books. Proficient writers can flexibly move among most, if not all, of these formats. Proficient writers are also able to move among purposes that range from writing solely for themselves (as in a personal diary) to communicating with an external audience.

Despite the real-world need for flexibility in writing skill, classroom instruction sometimes overemphasises certain forms of writing over others. For example, many students are taught a specific and quite rigid structure for writing an essay, commonly known as the "five-paragraph essay." Skilled writers, however, have more than that single structure to draw on when approaching a writing task. They have a variety of forms, strategies, knowledge, and skills at their disposal that they can apply flexibly to achieve their writing goals. Further, some teachers may overemphasize correct grammar or spelling at the expense of the expression of ideas. Excellent instruction in writing not only emphasises correctness of forms and conventions, but also instills in writers the command of a wide variety of forms, genres, styles, and tones, and the ability to adapt to different contexts and purposes.

Writing plays two distinct roles in school. First, it is a skill that draws on subskills and processes such as handwriting and spelling; a rich knowledge of vocabulary; mastery of the conventions of punctuation, capitalisation, word usage, and grammar; and the use of strategies (such as planning, evaluating, and revising text). All are necessary for the production of coherently organised essays containing well-developed and pertinent ideas, supporting examples, and appropriate detail. This role can be characterised as "learning to write." Second, writing is a means to extend and deepen students' knowledge; it acts as a tool for learning subject matter. This role is called "writing to learn." In fact, the roles of learning to write and of writing to learn are interdependent. Using writing tasks to learn content offers students opportunities to expand their knowledge of vocabulary; to strengthen the planning, evaluating, and revising process; and to practice grammar, spelling, punctuation, modes of argumentation, and technical writing.

8.2. Effective Writing Instruction

Writing proficiency develops over time. It begins as a kind of free association of ideas that a reader may find difficult to follow. From this comes a growing knowledge of stylistic conventions and more sophisticated uses of processes for planning, evaluating, and revising. Development continues with compositions marked by awareness of an audience and writing as a more unified and productive craft. Finally, at the most advanced stage, writing becomes a personal tool for transforming one's own experiences and knowledge. As they become more proficient writers, students move gradually from "knowledge-telling" to "knowledge-transformation". Knowledge-telling is most typical of less proficient writers and involves writing content that could in principle also be conveyed orally. Knowledge-transformation is more complex; the writing process is used as a way to extend ideas and reasoning and as a vehicle for the development of knowledge, philosophical ideas, and personal awareness.

Effective writing instruction acknowledges that the smooth deployment of the higher-level writing strategies needed to plan, generate, and revise text depends on easy use of lower-level skills such as handwriting, keyboarding, spelling, grammar and punctuation, and access to appropriate vocabulary. It will be harder for students to utilise strategies to write a coherent summary or persuasive essay if they are not fluent in the lower-level skills. At the same time, students who have difficulty with either lower-level writing skills or higher-level writing strategies will find it difficult to write to learn.

Although writing instruction has been researched much less often than reading instruction, it is an equally important component of literacy proficiency and encompasses, in itself, an extremely complex set of skills. The rich nature of the practice of writing and its relative neglect in instructional research make it inevitable that a whole compendium of possible approaches has not yet been studied. Research is clearly needed not only to identify additional effective practices that already exist but to develop new ones.

New practices in writing instruction have recently arisen and require investigation. For example, teachers have begun to use rubrics to teach students to reflect on and evaluate the quality of their own writing. The levelled lists of writing qualities or traits provided in a rubric give students tangible evaluation criteria. This approach is gaining support among educators. Vocabulary instruction in the context of writing is another practice that has been increasing recently and may be an effective procedure for improving students' writing.

8.3. Effective Practices in Teaching Writing

Ideally, writing teachers are practicing writers. By sharing their writing-particularly when it's in draft form-teachers model respect for themselves, for their students, and for the act of writing itself. They communicate that they are part of the writing community in the classroom and in the world at large and that they feel safe sharing this part of themselves.

8.3.1. Organise for Writing

Though teachers will be flexible to help their students and meet instructional goals, they also are thoughtful and systematic in organising for writing. Organising, of course, refers to planning the curriculum as well as the classroom activities and routines, practices established to help student develop as writers (and usually as readers and learners in a study area). Often teachers are required to address certain standards and assessment, and in organising for writing, they keep these curriculum needs/goals in mind.

8.3.1.1. Writing workshop

In terms of teaching practices, many teachers organise through a writing workshop structure, basically a studio approach in which student writers are engaged in developing their craft and are guided by a mature writer-the teacher. In the writing workshop, students are involved frequently in the writing process, though in some cases not all students necessarily are at the same place in that process. A writing workshop can have many components and kinds of activities, but here are some that are common:

- Directions from the teacher on the day's work or a brief review
- A block of time designated for planning, drafting, revising, editing, and sharing writing
- Time for reading and response to reading
- Mini-lessons, based on established curriculum, assessment, and, especially, students' needs as writers
- Time for students to receive responses to their writing-conferences with the teacher, classmates, and others
- Guidance in using appropriate resources for writing and learning
- Time for inquiry, as appropriate for the students' tasks
- Reflection and assessment

These are sample activities; not all of them necessarily occur daily. The teacher has a fundamental design, the workshop, but is flexible to meet the needs of students. During the workshop, the teacher organises the work, provides lessons and resources, guides and responds to students, models and facilitates. The amount of time devoted to writing workshop differs from teacher to teacher. Some conduct the workshop daily, others weekly, others at the end of a unit of study, etc. The main requirement is that students engage regularly in developing as writers-which usually includes developing as readers and as learners in a study area. Teachers across the grade levels and study areas can organise for writing in different modifications of a writing workshop structure.

8.3.1.2. Writer's notebook

Another useful tool in organising for writing is a writer's notebook. This tool is used during a writing workshop. The notebook, often a three-ring binder, may contain whatever the teacher and students think helpful. Some examples of contents are samples of the student's writing (works in progress, quick-write exercises, polished pieces, etc.); other samples that serve as examples of kinds of writing or of specific skills and strategies; conference records; planning forms and revision and editing checklists; instructional materials; resources on writing; items used in reflection and assessment; sentence combining exercises; etc. To model writing, the teacher may also keep a writer's notebook and share excerpts from it when appropriate.

8.3.1.3. A meaningful approach to writing

Teachers draw on their experience, on their understanding of their students, and on professional literature to select an approach that will be effective. Teachers might, for example, decide to use a multigenre approach or an approach based on immersion in literature. Here is a sampling of other approaches:

- Inquiry-based writing
- Writing based on study of popular media
- Writing relevant to a theme, issue, or problem or to an organising question for a unit of study Writing to gain experience with selected genres (for example, personal narrative, poem, editorial)
- Writing relevant to a project (for example, a study of community or school needs) Writing based on thinking processes (for example, comparing, evaluating, predicting, analysing, problem-solving)

8.3.1.4. Student choice of topic

Working within the selected approach, students complete one or more pieces of writing. Whatever the approach taken-and there are other options-the teacher bases the selection of the approach on what might be meaningful to students, a key principle in organising for writing.

8.3.2. Arrange for Meaningful-to-students Reasons to Write

This tenet for teaching writing is addressed also in the discussion of "organising for writing," but it is so important that it deserves a separate section. The assignment or the way students are led to write is a critical influence on their "will" to write and, thus, on their development as writers. As discussed above, teachers must think carefully about the approach they will use to arrange for students to write for meaningful purposes. True, it may not be easy to determine what will engage all students, and, true, some students are reluctant to write, but teachers should strive to "invite writing" to improve the odds that all students will be engaged and interested in writing.

8.3.2.1. Student choice and ownership

For at least some (and maybe all) assignments, providing students with choice, promoting ownership, and helping students draw on their own experience, interests, inquiry, etc., can engage students as writers. It is important to recognise that not all students have to write with exactly the same purpose or for the same audience. When students write about issues, needs, problems, or subjects they find important and relevant to their lives, we improve the odds for their engagement, as well as the likelihood that they will strive to write well. Under the teacher's guidance, students often conduct inquiry into matters of interest to them, generating ideas and questions and analysing problems and issues. The reason for writing is not merely to transcribe what others have said or recite what the teacher has taught. Inquiry may focus on personal experience, community issues, questions, themes, issues, problems, etc. From this inquiry, students develop writing to communicate their ideas for different purposes and audiences and in different forms.

8.3.2.2. Authentic writing and publishing

When students recognise that they are writing for authentic purposes and readers-when their writing is not simply a school exercise, when their writing is like that done in the "real world," when their writing will "go public" in some way-they likely will be more engaged as writers. Though teachers must prepare students for high-stakes assessment, students should perceive that the reason for doing the writing is more powerful than merely to prepare for the test or to receive a grade. Whenever possible, teachers should provide opportunities for publishing-posting student work on the wall, sharing finished writing with the class, mailing letters to intended audiences, doing presentations for younger students or for parents and families, creating a class publication, posting writing on the Web, etc. One additional benefit of publication is that it gives students a meaningful reason for revising and for editing for correctness.

8.3.3. Materials Written for a Variety of Purposes and Audiences

Though it may seem obvious, it is important to recognise that the experience of reading is a key way to help students gain familiarity with the ways writers work. Helping students "read like a writer" and respond to what they read also can make students aware of ways they, too, can write. The experience of reading is an important goal in itself and a focus on reading materials can help students develop as writers. However, teachers should not devote so much time to reading and analysis of texts that experience in writing is shortchanged.

8.3.3.1. Giving reading a role in the writing classroom

In organising for writing, teachers will determine how reading will play an important role in helping students develop as writers. Typically, the reading materials are used as models of writing or examples of genres, as a means of discussing a writer's strategies and techniques, as a means of stimulating students' interest and thinking about an issue or topic, and as resources to help students complete a task.

8.3.3.2. Using reading materials to model writing

Reading and talking about a variety of genres are important practices, and a variety of other practices can stem from this reading. Teachers can help students develop as writers by encouraging students to apply the techniques and characteristics of materials they read. Teachers can construct mini-lessons drawing on reading materials, and they can ask students to identify in the reading material important features they can apply in their own writing.

A very important practice is to lead students in reading and discussing samples of writing like those the students plan to write, including samples written by students. Many teachers maintain a file of such samples. Teachers often display samples or give students copies, and they lead the students in highlighting and annotating the samples as a preparation for their own writing.

8.3.3.3. Providing diverse reading materials

Standards for reading emphasise the importance of helping students read a variety of materials. It is important that the materials read are meaningful to the students, relevant to their lives, and useful in addressing their concerns and interests.

8.3.4. Write across the Curriculum and Grade Levels

Teachers across the curriculum may include different kinds of writing to help their students, for example, writing-to-learn practices like learning logs, response journals, quick writes, etc.; writing to demonstrate learning to the teacher, such as essays, reports, and responses to prompts; and writing in realistic forms for authentic purposes and readers. Writing regularly for different purposes will help students develop as writers and can also help them learn in any study area. Teachers include writing not merely to help students develop communication skills but to promote learning and thinking. Even students in the early grades can begin to write, using whatever they have learned about printed text along with their drawings to help them construct meaning. How much classroom time is devoted to writing and how frequently students write in their classrooms are matters the teacher will have to determine. It is especially important for young students to write frequently, perhaps each day. The point is that students need to engage in composing their thoughts, not merely complete skills exercises in preparation for some later day when they actually will write.

8.3.5. Students to have Constructive Response to their Writing

Students need to have response to their writing, and this response can occur throughout a writing cycle, can focus on any number of relevant matters, and can be offered in different ways by different people. Though providing response to students' writing is very important, teachers realise that not every piece of writing needs to be revised. Response focuses on developing the writer, not on "fixing" the piece of writing.

8.3.5.1. Achieving teaching goals through response

When teachers respond to student writing, they especially want to encourage students as writers, validating the writer and writing as important-perhaps the most important goal for response. They want to promote and preserve the student's ownership as a writer. Teachers also want to respond as a fellow writer and reader, modeling and conducting a conference as a conversation. They want to respond genuinely to the writer's ideas and experiences. They want to lead the student writer to talk, think, and make decisions. They want to describe what they see in the student's work, ask questions about content and form, provide suggestions or options, explain strategies or techniques, identify resources the student could use, and refer to mini-lessons.

8.3.5.2. Meeting the needs of student writers through response

What teachers decide to focus on in response will be based on curricular goals but mostly on the needs of their students as writers. The response might focus on such matters as strategies for revision, characteristics of different genres, criteria for good writing (e.g., organisation, support), techniques for persuasive writing, and, of course, specific features of the student's work. Teachers learn their students' needs as writers in a variety of ways-for example, through observing and listening to students engaged in writing, asking them to discuss their writing, and reading samples of students' writing. Some teachers learn about their students as writers by asking for letters of reflection or by maintaining charts with notes about students' work.

8.3.5.3. Providing selective responses

It is important that teachers do not focus on error alone when they respond to students' work. In fact, they realise that error can be a sign of risk-taking that is needed in progressing as a writer. Also, whether the response is from the teacher or from classmates, it should be selective. The teacher c.: students are not required to "cover everything."

8.3.5.4. Responding throughout the writing process

In the not-too-distant past, teachers responded only after the writing was "done." They "marked" the papers, often focusing only on errors, provided a grade, and went on to the next assignment. It is true that students should be expected and helped to edit their writing, but response should focus on more than error, and the purpose in responding to a students' writing is not solely to identify all the errors or problems. More often today, teachers provide response during the writing process-at any time: planning, drafting, revising, editing, publishing, reflecting.

Response does not have to occur in a formal conference setting; it can occur casually as the teacher looks over a student's shoulder or in an informal conversation held just before the start of class. Responses do not have to be long, either. In fact, sometimes an extended conference with a student can overload the student's circuits such that the student does not understand what to do or how to progress.

8.3.5.5. Using a variety of techniques for response

Teachers use a variety of techniques in arranging for response: teacher-student conferences, written notes to the student, peer conferences (pairs or small groups), response forms, whole-class response to a sample of writing (especially one done by a student from a former year), self-response notes in a writer's notebook, response provided by an older student or an adult, read-alouds, etc.

Students, of course, like to talk with each other, but merely asking students to get together and talk with each other about their writing usually is not enough. Students need guidance in responding to each other's writing. Teachers model good responses (and sometimes bad ones), they offer mini-lessons on response, and they lead students to define what truly helps them, so that response sessions are effective. Teachers also use forms and provide or ask students to create checklists that can serve as guides

8.3.6. Students to Collaborate as Writers, Thinkers, Learners

Teachers of writing take steps for students to work together throughout the writing process. In the past, when students wrote, the teacher often admonished, "Do your own work." The act of writing was viewed as a test that students were to complete with no assistance from others. Today, too, students sometimes are expected to write under test conditions, and it is true that teachers today want students to have ownership as writers, but they recognise that they can help student writers gain ownership and independence by working with classmates.

8.3.6.1. Collaboration techniques

Teachers use a variety of techniques to arrange for collaboration including:

- Arranging classroom furniture so students can work together
- Modeling and discussing effective methods of collaboration
- Helping students define and share with classmates what helps them as writers
- Providing checklists and forms to guide students
- Arranging for students to share and discuss drafts
- Organising writing partnerships or small groups

8.3.6.2. Collaboration guidelines

Students like to talk with each other, and they need to talk, so providing them a constructive means of doing so in a writing workshop helps engage the students and create a sense of community. Of course, the idea is not just to provide students with an opportunity to talk with each other, so teachers usually work with the students to establish the rules or principles that will apply to their collaboration, and teachers circulate to listen to the conversations and to guide students. Collaborating writers do not always agree, and students are taught to offer their ideas in constructive ways, in a tone that is that ot a conversation more than that of a debate or argument. Sometimes the work of one group is shared with the class, a demonstration of how writers are developing or solving problems.

Often, especially after a mini-lesson, teachers create specific tasks relevant to writing and lead students to work together on the task. Teachers also set forth certain specific objectives or ask questions that guide the collaboration, for instance, "Look at the examples we have discussed and help each other with the lead for your editorial. In ten minutes, let's meet in our celebration circle to discuss the before and after." Students are expected to think about content and form. Collaboration can have an important influence on students' growth as writers, and teachers will find many ways to promote collaboration, but it is essential that teachers and students affirm that individual writers should retain ownership of their work.

8.3.7. Conduct mini-lessons on writing

Though arranging for students to write and to develop as writers from this experience in writing is important, teachers also provide specific instruction, often through brief "minilessons" conducted in a writing workshop structure.

8.3.7.1. Choosing subjects for mini-lessons

In choosing what to address in mini-lessons, teachers refer to curriculum/assessment needs, their experience with their students, criteria for good writing, strategies used by writers, features of different genres, stylistic techniques, and, especially, their own students' needs as writers. For instance, if the teacher sees that students are having trouble creating effective leads, a mini-lesson is offered. The methods used will reflect awareness of different learning styles and students' backgrounds (educational, cultural, language). The mini-lesson is also an ideal vehicle for teaching usage and mechanics within the context of writing. The teacher can make sure that these lessons reflect the students' needs and that the students have ample opportunity to apply the lessons in a meaningful way.

8.3.7.2. Structuring mini-lessons

The anatomy of a mini-lesson will vary from time to time and teacher to teacher, but a typical structure is as follows: A separate skill, criterion, strategy, etc., is highlighted and explained, and sometimes students are given relevant resources or tools. Students are given a task in which they practice and talk about what has been taught. The teacher helps students understand approaches to the task, often by modeling or explaining procedures and strategies. Usually, students share what they have done in the task, discuss it, problem-solve, etc. Then, the skill or strategy is integrated into the student's own writing.

It is important that the mini-lesson not be perceived simply as isolated drill; it should be applied in the students' writing, writing for meaningful purposes. Teachers follow up to build on the lesson and also to see how well the students are able to integrate it into their own writing. When students are maintaining a writer's notebook, they might include in the notebook the resources, examples, practice exercises, quick writes, etc., from the mini-lesson. If including all this seems burdensome, then, of course, the items can be omitted.

References

Asher, J., "Motivating children and adults to acquire a second language", In J.W. Oller, Jr., and P.A. Richard-Amato (eds.) *Methods that work: A smorgasbord of ideas for language teachers,* Rowley, MA: Newbury House Publishers, Inc., 1983.

Bondy, E., "Children's definitions of reading: Products of an interactive process", *Paper presented at the annual meeting of the American Educational Research Association,* Chicago, Illinois, 1985.

Crandall, J., Spanos, G., Christian, D., Simich-Dudgeon, C., and Willetts, K., "Integrating language and content instruction for language minority students", Silver Spring, MD: National Clearinghouse for Bilingual Education, 1987.

Flores, B. and Garcia, E.A., "A collaborative learning and teaching experience using journal writing", *NABE Journal,* 1984.

Goodman, K., *What's whole in whole language,* Portsmouth, NH: Heinemann, 1986.

Goodman, K., Goodman, Y., and Hood, W.J., *The whole language evaluation book,* Portsmouth, NH: Heinemann, 1989.

Hamayan, E. and Pfleger, M., "Developing literacy in English as a second language: Guidelines for teachers of young children from non-literate backgrounds", Silver Spring, MD: National Clearinghouse for Bilingual Education, 1987.

Staton, J., Kreeft, J., and Gutstein, S., *Dialogue journals as a reading event*, Dialogue, 1985.

Ueland, B., *If you want to write*, Saint Paul, MN: Graywolf Press, 1987.

9

Teaching English Grammar

Grammar is central to the teaching and learning of languages. It is also one of the more difficult aspects of language to teach well. Some basic features of English language grammar structure are illogical or dissimilar to speakers of other languages and do not readily lend themselves to being well understood, even in context. Aspects of English language grammar that may offer exceptional challenge to EFL students include use of word order, determiners (this, that, these, those, a, an, the), prepositions (in, on, at, by, for, from, of), auxiliaries (do, be, have), conjunctions (but, so, however, therefore, though, although), interrogatives, intensifiers (some, any, few, more, too) and distinctions between modal verbs (can, could, would, should, may, might, must). Phrasal verbs also present considerable difficulty to Spanish speakers learning communicative English.

Some students also are logical or linguistically-biased thinkers who respond well to structured presentation of new material. Logical-Mathematical and Verbal-Linguistic intelligence learners are prime examples of those that would respond well to explicit grammar teaching in many cases. Although it is essential to teach elements of language and develop communicative abilities in our students, there is no one best way to introduce and provide practice in them. Young learners have more natural facility in acquisition, while adults may benefit substantially from more "formal" language learning. Learning styles and intelligence strengths are also a significant factor.

There are many generally accepted ways of introducing the sounds, structure and vocabulary of English, including colloquial forms of conversation and the four basic communication skills. Grammar provides for "communicative economy". Grammar teaching should be implicit, or explicit, as teaching / learning conditions may dictate helping to minimise the student response teachers fear most, "Teacher, I don't understand."

9.1. Grammar-centred Curriculum

The educational part called Language and language communication is taken as to one of the most important part in the educational programme. A high level of language culture belongs to the basic items of general education. Language learning supplies knowledge and skills that provide possibilities to receive several messages, it makes pupils understand these messages, it makes them express new things properly. Students should be able to use and enforce the results of their knowledge. Foreign and the second foreign language contribute to understanding and discovering the realities that are above the experience brought by mother tongue. These realities provide the basis of language communication and assumptions for communication in a scope of integrated Europe and the world.

The language acquisition helps to reduce a language barrier. It is useful for improving the mobility of the individuals both in their personal life and in their next professional carrier. The language acquisition enables pupils to know the differences of the traditions in foreign country. It intensifies the view of importance of reciprocal understanding and tolerance between countries. It facilitates cooperation between schools in the international projects.

The education in this area points to these key competences: pupils are expected:

- to receive language as a historical and cultural fact
- to know the historical and cultural development of the country and nation
- to make a positive view of mother tongue
- to use the language for receiving the information
- to require the main structures of communication between people
- to make a positive view of foreign language in a scope of multicultural communication

- to require the self confidence ior presenting in public
- to be able to read the literary texts
- to make a positive view of the classic literature and other arts
- to require an emotional and esthetic cognition

There have been increasing efforts to bring curricular objectives into alignment with language-functional aims and learner-behaviour specifications. It has been found that the goals of language-teaching programmes are often articulated in terms of "communicative competence", and much discussed in the pedagogic research literature are the so-called "communicative approaches" to language instruction. The fundamental premise of most such approaches is that the primary function of language is that of "communication". Certainly, the viability of any "communicative curriculum" will need to be linked in important ways to the validity of this premise; yet the premise itself represents a belief about language function.

Communication is a function of language-perhaps, according to some plausible but still undervised scale, its most important function. But communication does not appear to be the *only* function of language. Language is used for thought, for problem solving, for play, for dreaming, for displays of group solidarity, for deception, for certain specialised literary modes such as represented speech...,and possibly to fulfill an instinctive need for symbolic behaviour...; in fact, language plays an integral role in virtually every conceivable human activity. Now one might, of course, choose to call all these attributes and abilities "communication". But doing so, it seems to me, takes from the word "communication" any meaning other than "acting human".

According to William E. Rutherford there is nothing of intrinsic language organisation that can be identified, isolated, and abstracted away for curricular representation as the formal exponent of some set of "communicative functions". Grammar is in no sense amenable to such procedures, and this is as true for product as for process-oriented concepts of language form. These observations argue then against any centrality within the curriculum for systems of "communication" where decisions concerning grammatical focus are attendant upon "communicative" points of departure.

Letting language itself be at the centre of the pedagogical plan would seem at first glance to represent nothing new. Possible difficulties in accepting the value of a language-centred pedagogical plan would very likely stem from what we already know of so many such attempts in the past- attempts whose apparent failure to lead to desired goals has more recently, in the eyes of some language professionals, discredited the notion of any kind of curricular prominence for language organisation.

William E. Rutherford says:

> "There are two prime assumptions that are usually identifiable throughout the history of language-centred pedagogy. The first of these amounts to a belief about language, the second about teaching {learning}:

(1) the essence of language is an assemblage of hierarchically-arranged constructs;

(2) the essence of language teaching/learning is the direct imparting of those constructs by teacher to learner.

We can say that the learner has to be exposed to the data from which hypotheses may be formed and meaningful generalisations drawn. The exposure factor is a more crucial one than might be supposed; it becomes even more so where the classroom is the only source of target-language date. The need for making the data available to the learner therefore places a special burden of responsibility upon the language curriculum and language syllabus. The responsibility in curriculum planning has three parts to it:

1) some kinds of decision must be made as to what aspects of the grammatical system are the major sources for data from which the learner may ascertain the most formal generalisations.
2) choice of language content must be such as to ensure the sufficiently timely appearance of the grammatical aspects identified in (1).
3) great care and sensibility must be exercised that the pedagogical instruments maximise the probabilities for learner receptivity.

The complexity of language means that if someone learns language, it requires systematic direct contact with each of its possible constructions. It cannot be necessary for the learner to encounter the exhaustive set of target-language constructions. One of the primary responsibilities of the language-teaching curriculum would seem to become as close as possible an identification of the grammar properties of target-language lexicon. It is considered of crucial importance for learner projection to well-formed grammatical constructions.

The rules of grammar are about how words change and how they are put together into sentences. The knowledge of grammar also tells the learner what to do if he wants to put the some phrase into the sentence. Grammar should be called the way in which words change themselves and group together to make sentences. Each teacher should think about these facts and try to answer these questions before teaching grammar:

1) Children do not learn grammar rules when they acquire their first language, so do they need to learn the rules of grammar when they acquire the second language?
2) Pupils need or need not to be given details of grammar rules to study English successfully.
3) Should pupils get enough chance to practice using a language or should they learn grammar?
4) Should students be aware of grammatical information about the language?

A good teacher has several possibilities how to teach grammar. There is a number of techniques for presenting and practicing grammar. According to J.Harmer the grammatical information can be given to students in two major ways. The first one could be extremely covert and the second will be made extremely overt.

Covert grammar teaching means that grammatical facts are hidden from the students- even though they are learning the language. Students may be asked to do any activity where a new grammar is presented or introduced, but their attention will be drawn to this activity not to the grammar. Overt grammar teaching means that the teacher actually provides the students grammatical rules and explanations-the information is openly presented. With overt teaching grammatical rules are explicitly given to students, but with covert teaching students are simply asked to work with new language to absorb grammatical information which will help them to acquire the language as a whole.

The teaching of grammar is likely to be fairly covert since the main aim is to get students to use language as much as possible. On the other hand students at intermediate levels should be involved in more communicative activities and should have less grammar teaching. The teaching grammar would probably be more overt. Then advanced students can actively study grammar in more overt ways.

9.1.1. Presentation

Presentation means that students are introduced to the form, meaning and use of a new piece of language (e.g. did for past simple in questions). Students can learn how to put the new syntax, words and sounds together. They learn grammar that they will need for their most important experience, applying it to themselves. It is useful to mention the personalisation, which means using a piece of grammar to say things which really mean something to learner. (e.g. using present simple to say what he does). Presentation can take place using personalisation immediately, teacher uses the students and their lives to introduce a new language (e.g. personal questions). Personalisation can be the final part of a presentation which is done through the use of texts or pictures (e.g. using a situation in daily life, menu in a restaurant).

J. Harmer speaks about some characteristics of a good presentation that should be mentioned here:

– a good presentation should be clear (no difficulties in understanding for learner)
– a good presentation should be efficient (students can manipulate the new language)
– a good presentation should be lively and interesting (to get interest for students, their involving during a presentation)
– a good presentation should be appropriate (not put so much information)

– a good presentation should be productive (the introduced situation should allow students to make many sentences or questions with a new language)

We have said that a good presentation should be clear, efficient, lively and interesting, appropriate and productive. These can be fulfilled by many ways that are given to students by teacher. It is only up to teacher how he, she introduces the new grammatical item. Then students repeat and use this new item. Discovery techniques are possible ways where students are given examples of language and then asked to find out how they work, it means to discover the grammar rules. Students find out how grammar is used in a text and they are actually acquiring a grammar rule. By this students' involving in the task of grammar acquisition teacher makes sure that they are concentrating fully, using their cognitive powers. Discovery techniques are not just the teacher telling what the grammar is. Students are actually discovering information for themselves.

There are various ways of doing practice techniques, which means that pupils do exercise through the techniques which get them to practice grammatical item. There will be mentioned four different types of oral practice and written practice too, which are described by J.Harmer.

1) Drills are often done with the whole class, students are given sentence with a new grammatical item and they are asked for right repetition. It is practiced as long as it is necessary for students to be able to say this structure in a proper way. The aim of drill is to give students rapid practice in using a structural item. Advantage is that the teacher can correct any mistakes, can encourage pupils to concentrate on difficulties. But this way is not very creative.
2) Interaction activities are the ways of language practicing which are more meaningful and more enjoyable. Pupils often work together in pairs or in groups. They exchange information in the purposeful and interesting way. They are given some materials (text, picture, map) and asked for some tasks when they use the grammatical item that is introduced. Disadvantage should be that the teacher has no control over all students. He, she can't be sure that all students understood the grammar.

3) Involving the personality is the way when pupils do the exercise and at the same time talk about themselves. They are asked to discuss things that involve their personality and to use this subject matter as a focus for grammar practice. Chain drill is one way of making a practice drill. It is closely drill but in more funny and enjoyable way. It is more interesting than usual, because students are asked for speaking about themselves.
4) Games are surely the most interesting and the most favourite way how to practice grammar. Games are very useful for grammar work. Students are given a new grammatical item through the game, which is exactly the most natural way especially for children. There are several types of grammar games that will be mentioned later in this work.

9.1.2. Testing Grammar

There are several types of tests. Teacher can test students' ability to speak or write, his reading or listening skills. Of course, written tests take less time and they are easier to administer. That's why most tests are based on written skills. This could cause some problems, because so much teaching in the classroom is based on oral work. Teacher should remember this fact and try to make the tests suitable for students. Good test shows both teacher and learner how well they are all doing. Teacher who writes tests should bear in mind the rules that are offered by J.Hamer:

- do not test what you have not taught
- do not test general knowledge
- do not introduce new techniques in tests
- do not just test accuracy
- do not forget to test the test

All grammar teaching should not be covert. Teacher should not always draw students' attention to grammatical facts and rules. Sometimes pupils should discover facts about grammar through problem solving activities and sometimes through practicing grammar. Teacher should not think that the only best kind of grammar practice is written grammar practice. Teacher should remember that it is not good to test grammar only with accuracy.

The main point in teaching grammar is based on the fact that children do not learn grammar when they acquire first language, so it could work when they learn the second language.

9.1.3. Error Correction

At all proficiency levels, learners produce language that is not exactly the language used by native speakers. Some of the differences are grammatical, while others involve vocabulary selection and mistakes in the selection of language appropriate for different contexts. In responding to student communication, teachers need to be careful not to focus on error correction to the detriment of communication and confidence building. Teachers need to let students know when they are making errors so that they can work on improving. Teachers also need to build students' confidence in their ability to use the language by focusing on the content of their communication rather than the grammatical form.

Teachers can use error correction to support language acquisition, and avoid using it in ways that undermine students' desire to communicate in the language, by taking cues from context.

9.2. Strategies for Learning Grammar

Language teachers and language learners are often frustrated by the disconnect between knowing the rules of grammar and being able to apply those rules automatically in listening, speaking, reading, and writing. This disconnect reflects a separation between declarative knowledge and procedural knowledge.

- Declarative knowledge is knowledge *about* something. Declarative knowledge enables a student to describe a rule of grammar and apply it in pattern practice drills.
- Procedural knowledge is knowledge of how to do something. Procedural knowledge enables a student to apply a rule of grammar in communication.

For example, declarative knowledge is what you have when you read and understand the instructions for programming the DVD player. Procedural knowledge is what you demonstrate when you program the DVD player. Procedural knowledge does not translate automatically into declarative knowledge; many native speakers can use their language clearly and correctly without being able to state the rules of its grammar. Likewise, declarative knowledge does not translate automatically into procedural knowledge; students may be able to state a grammar rule, but consistently fail to apply the rule when speaking or writing.

To address the declarative knowledge/procedural knowledge dichotomy, teachers and students can apply several strategies.

9.2.1. Relate knowledge needs to learning goals

Identify the relationship of declarative knowledge and procedural knowledge to student goals for learning the language. Students who plan to use the language exclusively for reading journal articles need to focus more on the declarative knowledge of grammar and discourse structures that will help them understand those texts. Students who plan to live in-country need to focus more on the procedural knowledge that will help them manage day to day oral and written interactions.

9.2.2. Apply higher order thinking skills

Recognise that development of declarative knowledge can accelerate development of procedural knowledge. Teaching students how the language works and giving them opportunities to compare it with other languages they know allows them to draw on critical thinking and analytical skills. These processes can support the development of the innate understanding that characterises procedural knowledge.

9.2.3. Provide plentiful, appropriate language input

Understand that students develop both procedural and declarative knowledge on the basis of the input they receive. This input includes both finely tuned input that requires students to pay attention to the relationships among form, meaning, and use for a specific grammar rule, and roughly tuned input that allows students to encounter the grammar rule in a variety of contexts.

9.2.4. Use Predicting Skills

Discourse analyst Douglas Biber has demonstrated that different communication types can be characterised by the clusters of linguistic features that are common to those types. Verb tense and aspect, sentence length and structure, and larger discourse patterns all may contribute to the distinctive profile of a given communication type. For example, a history textbook and a newspaper article in English both use past tense verbs almost exclusively. However, the newspaper article will use short sentences and a discourse pattern that alternates between subjects or perspectives. The history textbook will use complex sentences and will follow a timeline in its discourse structure. Awareness of these features allows students to anticipate the forms and structures they will encounter in a given communication task.

9.2.5. Limit Expectations for Drills

- Mechanical drills in which students substitute pronouns for nouns or alternate the person, number, or tense of verbs can help students memorise irregular forms and challenging structures. However, students do not develop the ability to use grammar correctly in oral and written interactions by doing mechanical drills, because these drills separate form from meaning and use. The content of the prompt and the response is set in advance; the student only has to supply the correct grammatical form, and can do that without really needing to understand or communicate anything.
- Communicative drills encourage students to connect form, meaning, and use because multiple correct responses are possible. In communicative drills, students respond to a prompt using the grammar point under consideration, but providing their own content. For example, to practice questions and answers in the past tense in English, teacher and students can ask and answer questions about activities the previous evening.

9.3. Developing Grammar Activities

Many courses and textbooks, especially those designed for lower proficiency levels, use a specified sequence of grammatical topics as their organising principle. When this is the case, classroom activities need to reflect the grammar point that is being introduced or reviewed. By contrast, when a course curriculum follows a topic sequence, grammar points can be addressed as they come up.

For curricula that introduce grammatical forms in a specified sequence, instructors need to develop activities that relate form to meaning and use.

- Describe the grammar point, including form, meaning, and use, and give examples (structured input)
- Ask students to practice the grammar point in communicative drills (structured output)
- Have students do a communicative task that provides opportunities to use the grammar point (communicative output)

For curricula that follow a sequence of topics, instructors need to develop activities that relate the topical discourse (use) to meaning and form.

- Provide oral or written input (audiotape, reading selection) that addresses the topic (structured input)
- Review the point of grammar, using examples from the material (structured input)
- Ask students to practice the grammar point in communicative drills that focus on the topic (structured output)
- Have students do a communicative task on the topic (communicative output)

When instructors have the opportunity to develop part or all of the course curriculum, they can develop a series of contexts based on the real world tasks that students will need to perform using the language, and then teach grammar and vocabulary in relation to those contexts. For example, students who plan to travel will need to understand public address announcements in airports and train stations. Instructors can use audiotaped simulations to provide input; teach the grammatical forms that typically occur in such announcements; and then have students practice by asking and answering questions about what was announced.

9.3.1. Textbook Grammar Activities

Textbooks usually provide one or more of the following three types of grammar exercises.

-- *Mechanical drills*: Each prompt has only one correct response, and students can complete the exercise without attending to meaning. For example: George waited for the bus this morning. He *will wait* for the bus tomorrow morning, too.
– *Meaningful drills*: Each prompt has only one correct response, and students must attend to meaning to complete the exercise. For example: Where are George's papers? *They* are *in his notebook. (Students* must understand the meaning of the question in order to answer, but only one correct answer is possible because they all know where George's papers are.)
– *Communicative drills,* described in Strategies for Learning Grammar

9.4. Challenges of Teaching Grammar

Grammar is often misunderstood in the language teaching field. The misconception lies in the view that grammar is a collection of arbitrary rules about static structures in the language. Further questionable claims are that the structures do not have to be taught, learners will acquire them on their own, or if the structures are taught, the lessons that ensue will be boring. Consequently, communicative and proficiency-based teaching approaches sometimes unduly limit grammar instruction.

9.4.1. Grammar is Acquired Naturally

It is true that some learners acquire second language grammar naturally without instruction. For example, there are immigrants to the United States who acquire proficiency in English on their own. This is especially true of young immigrants. However, this is not true for all learners. Among the same immigrant groups are learners who may achieve a degree of proficiency, but whose English is far from accurate. A more important question may be whether it is possible with instruction to help learners who cannot achieve accuracy in English on their own.

It is also true that learning particular grammatical distinctions requires a great deal of time even for the most skilled learners. Carol Chomsky showed that native English speakers were still in the process of acquiring certain grammatical structures in English well into adolescence. Thus, another important question is whether it is possible to accelerate students' natural learning of grammar through instruction.

9.4.2. A Collection of Meaningless Forms

This myth may have arisen because many people associate the term grammar with verb paradigms and rules about linguistic form. However, grammar is not unidimensional and not meaningless; it embodies the three dimensions of morphosyntax (form), semantics (meaning), and pragmatics (use). Despite their interdependence, however, they each offer a unique perspective on grammar. Consider the passive voice in English. It clearly has form. It is composed minimally of a form of the "be" verb and the past participle. Sometimes it has the preposition "by" before the agent in the predicate: (1) "The bank was robbed by the same gang that hijacked the armoured car." That the passive can occur only when the main verb is transitive is also part of its formal description.

The passive has a grammatical meaning. It is a focus construction, which confers a different status on the receiver or recipient of an action than it would receive in the active voice. For example, the bank in sentence (1) is differently focused than it would be in the active sentence: (2) "The same gang robbed the bank."

When or why do we use the passive? When the receiver of the action is the theme or topic, when we do not know who the agent is, when we wish to deliberately conceal the identity of the agent, when the agent is obvious and easily derivable from the context, when the agent is redundant, and so on. To use the English passive voice accurately, meaningfully, and appropriately, English as a second language students must master all three dimensions. This is true of any grammatical structure.

9.4.3. Grammar Consists of Arbitrary Rules

While there is some synchronic arbitrariness to grammar, not all of what is deemed arbitrary is so. If one adopts a broad enough perspective, it is possible to see why things are the way they are. Consider the following sentences: "There is the book missing." "There is a book missing". Grammar books will say that sentence is ungrammatical because sentences with existential "there" almost always take an indefinite noun phrase in the predicate. Why? The reason is not arbitrary. There is used to introduce new information, and the preferred position for new information is toward the end of a sentence. A noun phrase that contains new information is marked by the use of the indefinite article, "a" or "an," if it is a singular common noun, as in sentence.

9.4.4. Grammar is Boring

Teaching grammar does not mean asking students to repeat models in a mindless way, and it does not mean memorising rules. Such activities can be boring and do not necessarily teach grammar. This does not mean there is no place for drills, but drills should be used in a meaningful and purposeful way. For example, to practice past-tense yes/no sentences in English, the teacher may ask her students to close their eyes while she changes five things about herself. She takes off one shoe, takes off her watch, puts on her glasses, puts on her sweater, and takes off her ring. Teaching grammar in a way that engages students may require creativity, but the teaching need not and should not be boring.

9.4.5. Students have Different Learning Styles

Some people have a more analytical learning style than others. Students have different strengths and weaknesses. It is clear that all students can learn grammar as is evident from their mastery of their first language. As grammar is no different from anything else, it is likely that students will learn at different rates.

9.4.6. Grammar Structures are Learned One at a Time

This myth is demonstrably untrue. Teachers may teach one grammar structure at a time, and students may focus on one at a time, but students do not master one at a time before going on to learn another. There is a constant interaction between new interlanguage forms and old. Students may give the appearance of having learned the present tense, for example, but when the present progressive is introduced, often their mastery vanishes and their performance declines. This backsliding continues until the grammar they have internalised is restructured to reflect the distinct uses of the two tenses.

9.4.7. Sentence-level and Subsentence-level Phenomena

Grammar does operate at the sentence level and governs the syntax or word orders that are permissible in the language. It also works at the subsentence level to govern such things as number and person agreement between subject and verb in a sentence. However, grammar rules also apply at the suprasentential or discourse level.

9.4.8. Grammar and Vocabulary are Areas of Knowledge

While grammar can be thought of as static knowledge, it can also be considered a process. Language teachers would not be content if their students could recite all the rules of grammar but not be able to apply them. The goal is for students to be able to use grammar in an unselfconscious fashion to achieve their communicative ends. As with any skill, achieving this goal takes practice.

References

Bygate, M., Tonkyn, A., & Williams, E. (Eds.), *Grammar and the language teacher*, Hemel Hempstead, England: Prentice Hall, 1994.

Byrd, P., "Writing grammar textbooks: Theory and practice", *System*, 1994.

_______________ ., "Issues in the writing and publication of grammar textbooks", *Material writer's guide*, Boston: Heinle & Heinle, 1995.

Celce-Murcia, M., & Hilles, S., *Techniques and resources in teaching grammar*, Oxford: Oxford University Press, 1988.

Larsen-Freeman, D., "Teaching grammar", In M. Celce-Murcia (Ed.), *Teaching English as a second or foreign language*, (3rd ed.), Boston: Heinle & Heinle, 2001.

Larsen-Freeman, D., *Teaching language: From grammar to grammaring*, Boston: Heinle & Heinle, 2001.

Ur, P., *Grammar practice activities: A practical guide for teachers*, Cambridge: Cambridge University Press, 1988.

10

Practices of Teaching Reading

Reading is an activity with a purpose. A person may read in order to gain information or verify existing knowledge, or in order to critique a writer's ideas or writing style. A person may also read for enjoyment, or to enhance knowledge of the language being read. The purpose for reading also determines the appropriate approach to reading comprehension. A person who needs to know whether she can afford to eat at a particular restaurant needs to comprehend the pricing information provided on the menu, but does not need to recognise the name of every appetiser listed. A person reading poetry for enjoyment needs to recognise the words the poet uses and the ways they are put together, but does not need to identify main idea and supporting details. However, a person using a scientific article to support an opinion needs to know the vocabulary that is used, understand the facts and cause-effect sequences that are presented, and recognise ideas that are presented as hypotheses and givens.

10.1. Reading as a Process

Reading is an interactive process that goes on between the reader and the text, resulting in comprehension. The text presents letters, words, sentences, and paragraphs that encode meaning. The reader uses knowledge, skills, and strategies to determine what that meaning is.

Reader knowledge, skills, and strategies include:

- *Linguistic competence:* the ability to recognise the elements of the writing system; knowledge of vocabulary; knowledge of how words are structured into sentences
- *Discourse competence:* knowledge of discourse markers and how they connect parts of the text to one another

- *Sociolinguistic competence:* knowledge about different types of texts and their usual structure and content
- *Strategic competence:* the ability to use top-down strategies, as well as knowledge of the language (a bottom-up strategy)

The purpose(s) for reading and the type of text determine the specific knowledge, skills, and strategies that readers need to apply to achieve comprehension. Reading comprehension is thus much more than decoding. Reading comprehension results when the reader knows which skills and strategies are appropriate for the type of text, and understands how to apply them to accomplish the reading purpose.

Instructors want to produce students who, even if they do not have complete control of the grammar or an extensive lexicon, can fend for themselves in communication situations. In the case of reading, this means producing students who can use reading strategies to maximise their comprehension of text, identify relevant and non-relevant information, and tolerate less than word-by-word comprehension.

To accomplish this goal, instructors focus on the process of reading rather than on its product.

- They develop students' awareness of the reading process and reading strategies by asking students to think and talk about how they read in their native language.
- They allow students to practice the full repertoire of reading strategies by using authentic reading tasks. They encourage students to read to learn (and have an authentic purpose for reading) by giving students some choice of reading material.
- When working with reading tasks in class, they show students the strategies that will work best for the reading purpose and the type of text. They explain how and why students should use the strategies.
- They have students practice reading strategies in class and ask them to practice outside of class in their reading assignments. They encourage students to be conscious of what they're doing while they complete reading assignments.

- They encourage students to evaluate their comprehension and self-report their use of strategies. They build comprehension checks into in-class and out-of-class reading assignments, and periodically review how and when to use particular strategies.
- They encourage the development of reading skills and the use of reading strategies by using the target language to convey instructions and course-related information in written form: office hours, homework assignments, test content.
- They do not assume that students will transfer strategy use from one task to another. They explicitly mention how a particular strategy can be used in a different type of reading task or with another skill.

10.2. Stages in teaching Reading

Reading for second or foreign language learners of English as an acquisition process in three stages:

10.2.1. Elementary Reading

The students are exposed to the association of the letters of the English alphabet with their relevant sounds in appropriate contexts. In this process, they discover the relationship between the alphabet and the spoken language. Students are given groups of simple words, phrases, and sentences with focus on one or two letters and their combinations. They are introduced to the correspondence between the individual letters and their combinations in graded steps. They come to internalise, in an inductive manner, the possibilities of sound values for each letter, or combination of letters. Emphasis is thus on decoding graphic information from the words, phrases, and sentences. Based on what they have been exposed to, students begin to read new combinations of vocabulary and sentence-level structures. They develop an ability to predict the sound values represented by the letters and their combinations in contexts.

10.2.2. Intermediate Reading

The intermediate reading stage fosters interest in reading, and develops the actual reading skill practiced throughout one's life beyond mastering the association between letters and sounds. Students no more read aloud. They are comfortable with predicting the sound values of letters and their combinations, and they begin to read for the purposes for which they originally enrolled themselves in the class.

10.2.3. Advanced Reading

Most students are quite satisfied with what they have accomplished in the intermediate stage. However, reading is a continuing process, and they need to be introduced to the reading of authentic materials for specific purposes. Stories re-told, and abridged and adapted versions are the focus in intermediate level. But at the advanced level originals are presented.

10.2.3.1. Reading readiness

Reading readiness exercises help students to recognise and read the letters and words. Reading readiness exercises may or may not use linguistic materials, but whatever materials are used, these should be easy to handle and are familiar to the students. The goal of reading readiness exercises is to help foster a congenial atmosphere for learning reading and to develop some favorable attitude toward reading.

Visual Discrimination, Auditory Discrimination, and Memory Training are some of the reading readiness exercises given to the students.

Visual discrimination

Directions like same, different, top, bottom, middle, first, second and last referring to objects, letters, and words are presented in these exercises. In English, for example, the students need to distinguish between p and q, between d and p, and so on.

Names and general shapes of the letters of the alphabet that English uses, different forms of the same letters (upper and lower case forms, etc.), ability to tell whether two letters or groups of letters are the same or different are all focused in these exercises.

Some possible discriminations: What is at the top, at the bottom, in the middle of the page? Which object is the first, the second, the last? Are any of the objects, letters, or words the same as the one in the box? Pair the capital and lower case letters as shown in the example.

Auditory discrimination

Although the auditory discrimination exercises are part of the preparation for listening, these need to be presented even as reading readiness exercises. This is important for those students who hear or repeat a sound persistently wrong. There is a close relationship between the auditory image of the word and its reading and reproduction in writing. Each word has its own auditory image, and this auditory image should be retrieved correctly in the reading process. Otherwise it could lead to misreading and misspelling.

Memory training

This training helps students to hold something in the mind for a length of time.

Some exercises:

- Repeat the first sentence of three after all have been heard.
- Give the order of events in a story heard.
- Name as many of the objects from memory as possible after a picture, or an array of objects, has been shown for a limited time and then removed from sight.
- Reassemble a picture series in the order first shown.

These exercises help the students to focus on the form of the words (spelling). Once the form is internalised, it is possible for the students to predict what the other parts of a word would be when he/she is given a word. In other words, he/she does not go from one letter to another in his/her reading process. He/she is able to predict and thus read the word in its entirety. This helps increase the reading speed also. Remember that although spelling a word is an important first step towards reading, it is only a first step. Spelling a word must be dropped in favor of reading a word in its entirety.

A student may be said to be in control of the basics when he:

- regularly makes appropriate eye movements for English.

- recognises and discriminates among the vowel and consonant sounds in English.
- associates vowel and consonant sounds with letters.
- recognises and discriminates among consonant blends and consonant combinations.
- recognises and discriminates among vowel combinations.
- recognises vowel sounds with /r/.
- recognises selected sight words.
- recognises rhyming words when not spelled with the same letter pattern.
- recognises upper- and lower-case letters and the basic punctuation marks.

10.2.4. Aloud Reading

Students do not learn to read by reading aloud. A person who reads aloud and comprehends the meaning of the text is coordinating word recognition with comprehension and speaking and pronunciation ability in highly complex ways. Students whose language skills are limited are not able to process at this level, and end up having to drop one or more of the elements. Usually the dropped element is comprehension, and reading aloud becomes word calling: simply pronouncing a series of words without regard for the meaning they carry individually and together. Word calling is not productive for the student who is doing it, and it is boring for other students to listen to.

- There are two ways to use reading aloud productively in the language classroom. Read aloud to your students as they follow along silently. You have the ability to use inflection and tone to help them hear what the text is saying. Following along as you read will help students move from word-by-word reading to reading in phrases and thought units, as they do in their first language.
- Use the "read and look up" technique. With this technique, a student reads a phrase or sentence silently as many times as necessary, then looks up (away from the text) and tells you what the phrase or sentence says. This encourages students to read for ideas, rather than for word recognition.

10.3. Teaching the Mechanics of Reading

Essentially there are two kinds of methods which take care of the mechanics of reading: the whole word method, and the linguistic method. Students are given the whole word to read in the first method, whereas they are first introduced to the elements which constitute the word in the second method, and then asked to combine them. Signs such as Exit, Entrance, Gentlemen, Ladies, No Entrance, Cafeteria, Fifteen Items or less, Open, Closed, etc., will be given without any analysis of the constituent elements. Students will associate the entire sound(s) with the entire written form.

In the linguistic method, students are introduced to the sound-symbol correspondences first in the word, and then they are enabled to combine the sounds to produce the word. It is important that second/foreign language learners of English are taught to recognise sight vocabulary in an automatic manner, without spelling such vocabulary. There are about two to three hundred words in English which account for a good part of all the words used on a written page. There are also set phrases in English which function as sight vocabulary. The students should be enabled to recognise these also as sight vocabulary.

Remember that in the initial stages of reading it is always useful to insist on students reading aloud. This helps them improve their reading pronunciation, and develop a sensitivity to how words are pronounced in English. When they come across a new word, this reading aloud practice will help them to attempt more or less a correct pronunciation of the word.

The teachers have been using a variety of materials to help students read with better pronunciation, and to motivate them to read in order to meet their needs. They often tend to use materials which the second/foreign language learner of English may have to use frequently, materials such as public announcements, invitations to parties and weddings, telephone messages, guidelines to perform a task, instructions to assemble toys, recipe, etc. The materials which focus on the learners' survival needs, social needs, and personal needs are presented to them for reading. Reading Games which use catchy phrases in ads, T-shirts, campaign buttons, posters, stickers, etc., are presented to the beginning reader, even when he/she is struggling to master the mechanics of decoding the English alphabet.

Once the reading mechanics relating to the decoding of the alphabet is well established, once the mastery of adequate sight vocabulary is also accomplished, the reading texts may focus on familiarising the students with the phrase and sentence structure in the reading materials. Students need to learn the differences between a phrase and a sentence in the texts to read. While the sentence is the required minimal unit in written English, phrases function as breath groups. "Phrase reading exercises can be useful in weaning the reader from word-for-word reading, and can help increase speed." Some of the exercises which can be used to develop phrase reading are: "repeat-and-copy exercises, the use of flash cards, lists on the blackboard, matching phrases, etc." Focusing on phrases and sentences for reading will help students not only to foster better speed in reading, but it will aid them in learning more English structures for practical purposes.

The students must be helped to develop a sensitivity to the English word structure. For this, the students will begin reading the most regular and the most productive word patterns in English, and then they will be exposed to the reading of irregular forms. If they internalise the regular patterns they will begin to look at the derived and inflected words such as past tense forms, adjectivals, adverbs, etc., as single entities. The irregular patterns will be learned as sight words or phrases.

10.3.1. Reading Lesson

There are four steps followed in a reading lesson:

1. Introduction. The teacher explains the purpose for reading the target passage, gives the students a setting for the text to be read, presents a background of appropriate information for the text to be read, and selects and introduces the new vocabulary necessary to comprehend the main ideas in the text.
2. The reading. This is generally an oral exercise for the beginners, usually consisting of listening to the passage read aloud, or listening and following along. Later on reading is silent.
3. Comprehension tasks.
4. Review and related exercises.

The following behavioral steps may be followed in the class:

1. Teacher reads while students listen.
2. Discussion.
3. Teacher reads while students listen and read along.
4. Discussion.
5. Student(s) read aloud (in small groups or in dyads).
6. Discussion.
7. Students read silently, or practice reading aloud individually.
8. Three types of questions are employed for discussion: information (what, when, where, who, how many, etc.), inferential (Did Juan know English when he came to the United States? How do we know? Does Juan know how to drive?), interpretive (questions relating to author's opinion, reader's judgment concerning the content of the article, etc.).

10.3.2. Silent Reading

Adult students tend to read silently even in their beginning level. This must be discouraged. There is a need to develop an association between the form (words, phrases, and sentences) and its corresponding sound representation. This is better achieved by oral reading. Success with oral reading helps also the success with speaking. So, encourage your adult students to read aloud as often as possible. Towards the end of the elementary or beginner's level, students may be allowed to read silently to some extent.

To develop silent reading, start with phrase reading. Encourage your students to read the phrases at a single stretch, not going from word to word. Flash cards with phrases may be shown for them to read the individual phrases at a single stretch. Flash the card for a brief while and they should catch the phrase and read it. Choose the phrases from the text or from common expressions frequently used in spoken English.

Show them only a partially written phrase and encourage them to guess the full phrase. Rearrange the words in a phrase and ask them to give the correct phrase from memory. Give them a list of words and ask them to put them together into as many phrases as they can. Or specify a number. Give them two or three sentences and ask them to read silently and time the reading. Then give them another set of sentences of same length and ask them to read silently, and time their reading. Step by step, increase the number of sentences. And increase the number of words in individual sentences. Time their reading.

10.3.3. Extensive Reading

To help foster extensive reading, students should be given materials that are interesting to the students. The most important intermediate reading skills are:

- Reading with incomplete information (Reading a passage with a sizable number of unfamiliar vocabulary items).
- Organising for careful reading (skimming and scanning).
- Organising information (specific time to preview).
- Reading critically.
- Developing effective personal reading strategies.
- Setting effective reading speeds for different kinds of reading.

Success at the intermediate level of reading depends a lot on the initiative the learner takes and the positive attitude he or she has towards reading. The learner should recognise the pivotal role reading plays in improving his/her diction and pronunciation, even as it helps him/her internalise the structures of English. The learner should find for himself or herself how studious reading habits help him/her perform better in English at all the levels - speaking, listening, and writing. Reading materials are abundant in all the surroundings and it is for the learner to take advantage of all these reading materials in his/her surroundings.

10.4. Developing Reading Skills

10.4.1. Reading Strategies

Language instructors are often frustrated by the fact that students do not automatically transfer the strategies they use when reading in their native language to reading in a language they are learning. Instead, they seem to think reading means starting at the beginning and going word by word, stopping to look up every unknown vocabulary item, until they reach the end. When they do this, students are relying exclusively on their linguistic knowledge, a bottom-up strategy. One of the most important functions of the language instructor, then, is to help students move past this idea and use top-down strategies as they do in their native language.

Effective language instructors show students how they can adjust their reading behavior to deal with a variety of situations, types of input, and reading purposes. They help students develop a set of reading strategies and match appropriate strategies to each reading situation.

Strategies that can help students read more quickly and effectively include

- *Previewing:* reviewing titles, section headings, and photo captions to get a sense of the structure and content of a reading selection
- *Predicting:* using knowledge of the subject matter to make predictions about content and vocabulary and check comprehension; using knowledge of the text type and purpose to make predictions about discourse structure; using knowledge about the author to make predictions about writing style, vocabulary, and content
- *Skimming and scanning:* using a quick survey of the text to get the main idea, identify text structure, confirm or question predictions
- *Guessing from context:* using prior knowledge of the subject and the ideas in the text as clues to the meanings of unknown words, instead of stopping to look them up
- *Paraphrasing:* stopping at the end of a section to check comprehension by restating the information and ideas in the text

Instructors can help students learn when and how to use reading strategies in several ways.

- By modeling the strategies aloud, talking through the processes of previewing, predicting, skimming and scanning, and paraphrasing. This shows students how the strategies work and how much they can know about a text before they begin to read word by word.

- By allowing time in class for group and individual previewing and predicting activities as preparation for in-class or out-of-class reading. Allocating class time to these activities indicates their importance and value.
- By using cloze (fill in the blank) exercises to review vocabulary items. This helps students learn to guess meaning from context.
- By encouraging students to talk about what strategies they think will help them approach a reading assignment, and then talking after reading about what strategies they actually used. This helps students develop flexibility in their choice of strategies.

When language learners use reading strategies, they find that they can control the reading experience, and they gain confidence in their ability to read the language.

10.4.2. Reading to Learn

Reading is an essential part of language instruction at every level because it supports learning in multiple ways.

- *Reading to learn the language*: Reading material is language input. By giving students a variety of materials to read, instructors provide multiple opportunities for students to absorb vocabulary, grammar, sentence structure, and discourse structure as they occur in authentic contexts. Students thus gain a more complete picture of the ways in which the elements of the language work together to convey meaning.
- *Reading for content information*: Students' purpose for reading in their native language is often to obtain information about a subject they are studying, and this purpose can be useful in the language learning classroom as well. Reading for content information in the language classroom gives students both authentic reading material and an authentic purpose for reading.

- *Reading for cultural knowledge and awareness*: Reading everyday materials that are designed for native speakers can give students insight into the lifestyles and worldviews of the people whose language they are studying. When students have access to newspapers, magazines, and Web sites, they are exposed to culture in all its variety, and monolithic cultural stereotypes begin to break down.

When reading to learn, students need to follow four basic steps:

1. *Figure out the purpose for reading*. Activate background knowledge of the topic in order to predict or anticipate content and identify appropriate reading strategies.
2. Attend to the parts of the text that are relevant to the identified purpose and ignore the rest. This selectivity enables students to focus on specific items in the input and reduces the amount of information they have to hold in short-term memory.
3. Select strategies that are appropriate to the reading task and use them flexibly and interactively. Students' comprehension improves and their confidence increases when they use top-down and bottom-up skills simultaneously to construct meaning.
4. Check comprehension while reading and when the reading task is completed. Monitoring comprehension helps students detect inconsistencies and comprehension failures, helping them learn to use alternate strategies.

10.5. Developing Reading Activities

Developing reading activities involves more than identifying a text that is "at the right level," writing a set of comprehension questions for students to answer after reading, handing out the assignment and sending students away to do it. A fully-developed reading activity supports students as readers through prereading, while-reading, and post-reading activities. As you design reading tasks, keep in mind that complete recall of all the information in a text is an unrealistic expectation even for native speakers. Reading activities that are meant to increase communicative competence should be success oriented and build up students' confidence in their reading ability.

10.5.1. Use Pre-reading Activities

The activities you use during pre-reading may serve as preparation in several ways. During pre-reading you may:

- Assess students' background knowledge of the topic and linguistic content of the text
- Give students the background knowledge necessary for comprehension of the text, or activate the existing knowledge that the students possess
- Clarify any cultural information which may be necessary to comprehend the passage
- Make students aware of the type of text they will be reading and the purpose(s) for reading
- Provide opportunities for group or collaborative work and for class discussion activities

Pre-reading activities are most important at lower levels of language proficiency and at earlier stages of reading instruction. As students become more proficient at using reading strategies, you will be able to reduce the amount of guided pre-reading and allow students to do these activities themselves.

10.5.2. Match While-reading Activities

In while-reading activities, students check their comprehension as they read. The purpose for reading determines the appropriate type and level of comprehension.

- When reading for specific information, students need to ask themselves, have I obtained the information I was looking for?
- When reading for pleasure, students need to ask themselves, Do I understand the story line/sequence of ideas well enough to enjoy reading this?
- When reading for thorough understanding (intensive reading), students need to ask themselves, Do I understand each main idea and how the author supports it? Does what I'm reading agree with my predictions, and, if not, how does it differ? To check comprehension in this situation, students may

– Stop at the end of each section to review and check their predictions, restate the main idea and summarise the section
– Use the comprehension questions as guides to the text, stopping to answer them as they read

10.5.3. Textbook Reading Activities

Many language textbooks emphasize product (answers to comprehension questions) over process (using reading skills and strategies to understand the text), providing little or no contextual information about the reading selections or their authors, and few if any pre-reading activities. Newer textbooks may provide pre-reading activities and reading strategy guidance, but their one-size-fits-all approach may or may not be appropriate for your students.

You can use the guidelines for developing reading activities given here as starting points for evaluating and adapting textbook reading activities. Use existing, or add your own, pre-reading activities and reading strategy practice as appropriate for your students. Don't make students do exercises simply because they are in the book; this destroys motivation.

Another problem with textbook reading selections is that they have been adapted to a predetermined reading level through adjustment of vocabulary, grammar, and sentence length. This makes them more immediately approachable, but it also means that they are less authentic and do not encourage students to apply the reading strategies they will need to use outside of class.

10.5.4. Integrating Reading Strategies

Instruction in reading strategies is not an add-on, but rather an integral part of the use of reading activities in the language classroom. Instructors can help their students become effective readers by teaching them how to use strategies before, during, and after reading.

Before reading: Plan for the reading task

– Set a purpose or decide in advance what to read for
– Decide if more linguistic or background knowledge is needed

- Determine whether to enter the text from the top down (attend to the overall meaning) or from the bottom up (focus on the words and phrases)

During and after reading: Monitor comprehension

- Verify predictions and check for inaccurate guesses
- Decide what is and is not important to understand
- Reread to check comprehension
- Ask for help

After reading: Evaluate comprehension and strategy use

- Evaluate comprehension in a particular task or area
- Evaluate overall progress in reading and in particular types of reading tasks
- Decide if the strategies used were appropriate for the purpose and for the task
- Modify strategies if necessary

10.5.5. Authentic Materials and Approaches

For students to develop communicative competence in reading, classroom and homework reading activities must resemble (or be) real-life reading tasks that involve meaningful communication. They must therefore be authentic in three ways.

1. *The reading material must be authentic*: It must be the kind of material that students will need and want to be able to read when traveling, studying abroad, or using the language in other contexts outside the classroom.

   When selecting texts for student assignments, remember that the difficulty of a reading text is less a function of the language, and more a function of the conceptual difficulty and the task(s) that students are expected to complete. Simplifying a text by changing the language often removes natural redundancy and makes the organisation somewhat difficult for students to predict. This actually makes a text more difficult to read than if the original were used. Rather than simplifying a text by changing its language, make it more approachable by eliciting students' existing knowledge in pre-reading discussion, reviewing new vocabulary before reading, and asking students to perform tasks that are within their competence, such as skimming to get the main idea or scanning for specific information, before they begin intensive reading.

2. *The reading purpose must be authentic*: Students must be reading for reasons that make sense and have relevance to them. "Because the teacher assigned it" is not an authentic reason for reading a text.

   To identify relevant reading purposes, ask students how they plan to use the language they are learning and what topics they are interested in reading and learning about. Give them opportunities to choose their reading assignments, and encourage them to use the library, the Internet, and foreign language newsstands and bookstores to find other things they would like to read.

3. *The reading approach must be authentic*: Students should read the text in a way that matches the reading purpose, the type of text, and the way people normally read. This means that reading aloud will take place only in situations where it would take place outside the classroom, such as reading for pleasure. The majority of students' reading should be done silently.

References

Ackersold, J. A., & Field, M. L., *From reader to reading teacher: Issues and strategies for second language classrooms*, New York: Cambridge University Press, 1997.

Anderson, N., *Exploring second language reading: Issues and strategies*, Boston, MA: Heinle & Heinle, 1999.

Bernhardt, E., *Reading development in a second language*, Norwood, NJ: Ablex, 1991.

Day, R. R., & Bamford, J., *Extensive reading in the second language classroom*, New York: Cambridge University Press, 1998.

Devine, J., "The role of metacognition in second language reading and writing", In J. G. Carson & I. Leki (Eds.), *Reading in the composition classroom*, Boston, MA: Heinle & Heinle, 1993.

Eskey, D., "Reading and the teaching of L2 reading", *TESOL Journal*, 2002.

Glazer, S. M., *Reading comprehension: Self-monitoring strategies to develop independent readers,* New York: Scholastic Professional Books, 1992.

Grellet, F., *Developing reading skills: A practical guide to reading comprehension exercises,* Cambridge: Cambridge University Press, 1981.

Silberstein, S., *Techniques and resources in teaching reading,* New York: Oxford University Press, 1994.

Swaffar, J., Arens, K., & Byrnes, H., *Reading for meaning: An integrated approach to language learning,* Englewood Cliffs, NJ: Prentice-Hall, 1991.

Urquhart, A. H., & Weir, C., *Reading in a second language: Process, product, and practice,* New York: Longman, 1998.

11

Teaching and Developing Vocabulary

For the first five years or so of their lives, children are involved in the process of acquiring a meaning/oral vocabulary—words that they understand when they hear them and that they can use in their speech. During this period, children have essentially no literate vocabularies. Most children acquire reading and writing skills upon entering school. They need to acquire a basic knowledge of how printed letters relate to the sounds of spoken words and how printed words relate to spoken words. Being able to translate or transcode print into speech allows children to use what they know about meaning/oral vocabulary for their literate vocabulary. So for very young children, their meaning vocabularies are much larger than their literate vocabularies.

The acquisition of decoding skills leads to rapid expansion of literate vocabularies by allowing children to transcode their meaning vocabularies into their literate vocabularies. This is so much the case that for older students and for adults our literate vocabularies are probably larger than our meaning vocabularies. We tend to have a larger group of words that we use in reading and writing than we use in our own speech. This is because written language is more formal, more complex, and more sophisticated than spoken language.

11.1. Reading Vocabulary

Young children naturally learn to communicate through listening and speaking. In order to make the transition to communicating through reading and writing, they need a large meaning vocabulary and effective decoding skills. An effective decoding strategy allows students not only to identify printed words accurately but to do so rapidly and automatically.

There is no question that people who have large speaking vocabularies generally tend to have large listening, reading, and writing vocabularies; likewise people who are limited in one of these aspects are likely limited in other aspects as well. We have seen that this close relationship does not exist in preliterate children. Also, some children who develop large reading vocabularies may not use that vocabulary in their writing without teacher help and guidance. However, in the years during which children develop as readers and writers, there is an increasingly high relationship among all four aspects of vocabulary—listening, speaking, reading, and writing. Fostering improvement in one aspect has the potential for fostering improvement in another. Therefore, one responsibility of teachers is to help children transfer vocabulary skills from one form to another.

While the dependence of both general achievement and reading achievement on vocabulary growth has been clearly established for decades, those findings do not appear to have been put into practice. The effects of the lack of attention to vocabulary instruction, however, may not manifest themselves in the earliest grades where tests of reading achievement tend to contain passages that have simple content and common vocabulary. While most students who succeed in reading in the early grades continue to achieve well, some do not.

Indeed, a commonly reported phenomenon in reading test results is for achievement to be good through second or third grade and to falter thereafter. This drop off in achievement seems very likely due to weaknesses in language development and background knowledge, which are increasingly required for reading comprehension beyond the early grades and for reading informational and content-area texts.

11.2. Teaching and Developing Vocabulary: A Comprehensive Approach

The amount of vocabulary that children need to acquire each year is staggering in scope, estimated to be about 3,000 words a year. Therefore, a comprehensive approach consisting of the following components needs to be in place.

— Use "instructional" read-aloud events.

- Provide direct instruction in the meanings of clusters of words and individual words.
- Systematically teach students the meaning of prefixes, suffixes, and root words.
- Link spelling instruction to reading and vocabulary instruction.
- Teach the effective, efficient, realistic use of dictionaries, thesauruses, and other reference works.
- Teach, model, and encourage the application of a word-learning strategy.
- Encourage wide reading.
- Create a keen awareness of and a deep interest in language and words.

11.2.1. Use Instructional Read-Aloud Events

The recommendation that parents and teachers read aloud to children is among the most popular recommendations in the field of reading. One very obvious way in which reading aloud to children can be expected to be beneficial is to increase their language and vocabulary skills. Indeed there is research to support this position.

11.2.2. Provide Direct Instruction in the Meanings of Words

Which words should be taught? In deciding which words to teach we have found it helpful to think about "levels" of vocabulary:

Level I Words: These are words that are used over and over in everyday speech. Since they are so frequently used in a variety of contexts, virtually all children learn them. Some examples of these words would be house, girl, cat, up, umbrella, etc. Level I words are sometimes referred to as "conversational speech." Children who are learning English as a second language will sometimes make progress with this level of vocabulary but have difficulty making progress with words at levels beyond this one.

Level II Words: These are words that are likely to be learned only through reading or through instruction. They have been referred to as the vocabulary of educated persons, as "academic vocabulary," and as "instructional vocabulary." They are words that are necessary for general success in school. Words such as perspective, generate, initiate, intermediate, calculation, etc. are possible examples.

Level III Words: These are words associated with a particular field of study or profession. These words make up the technical vocabulary or jargon of a field. Examples of Level III words from the field of reading instruction include the terms digraph, diphthong, schwa, metacomprehension, etc. As one might expect, some words such as calculation might be classified as either a Level II or Level III word or both.

Level IV Words: These are words that are interesting but so rare and esoteric that they are probably not useful even in most educational environments, and they are not associated with a field of study or profession. Examples are words that were but no longer are used: majuscule (a capital letter), xanthodont (one who has yellow teeth like a rodent), noctuary (an account of what happens in a night). Notice, however, that some Level IV words are useful for teaching morphological clues such as noct meaning "night" and dont or dent referring to teeth. Level IV words are also helpful for creating an interest in words and language.

11.2.3. Teaching the Meaning of Prefixes, Suffixes, and Root Words

The majority of English words have been created through the combination of morphemic elements, that is, prefixes and suffixes with base words and word roots. If learners understand how this combinatorial process works, they possess one of the most powerful understandings necessary for vocabulary growth. This understanding of how meaningful elements combine is defined as morphological knowledge because it is based on an understanding of morphemes, the smallest units of meaning in a language. In the intermediate grades and beyond, most new words that students encounter in their reading are morphological derivatives of familiar words. In recent years research has suggested some promising guidelines for teaching the meanings of prefixes, suffixes, and word roots as well as for the ways in which knowledge of these meaningful word parts may be applied. Word roots such as dict, spect, and struct are meaningful parts of words that remain after all prefixes and suffixes have been removed but that usually do not stand by themselves as words: prediction, inspection, contract.

In the primary grades students begin to explore the effects of prefixes such as un-, re-, and dis- on base words. In the intermediate grades students continue to explore prefixes and an increasing number of suffixes and their effects on base words: govern (verb) + -ment = government (noun). Common Greek and Latin roots begin to be explored, along with the effects of prefixes and suffixes that attach to them. These include, for example, chron ("time," as in chronology), tele ("distant, far" as in television), and fract ("break," as in fracture). Alarge proportion of the vocabulary of specific content areas is built on Greek and Latin elements. As this morphological knowledge develops, teachers can model how it may be applied to determining the meanings of unfamiliar words encountered in print.

11.2.4. Spelling Instruction to Reading and Vocabulary Instruction

Spelling knowledge applies not only to the ability to encode words during writing; importantly, it also underlies individuals' ability to decode words during the process of reading. Students' spelling knowledge is, therefore, a powerful foundation for their reading and their vocabulary development. Words that are related in meaning are often related in spelling, despite changes in sound. Among intermediate students, examination of how spelling patterns reflect meaning leads to vocabulary growth. To get a sense of how the connection works between spelling and meaning, examine the following words: bomb/ bombard; muscle/ muscular; compete/competition. Because the words in each pair are related in meaning, the spelling of the underlined sounds remains constant; although the sound that letters represent may change in related words, the spelling usually remains the same because it preserves the meaning relationship that these words share.

Once students understand the spelling-meaning relationships among words, they can learn how the spelling or structure of familiar words can be clues to the spelling and the meaning of unknown words, and vice-versa. For example, a student who spells condemn as condem in her spontaneous writing may be shown the word condemnation: This not only explains the so-called "silent" n in condemn but expands the student's vocabulary at the same time.

11.2.5. Teach the Use of Dictionaries, Thesauruses, and Other Reference Works

Exploring dictionary entries can be one important and effective component of understanding a word deeply. The entries can also help students determine the precise meaning of a word.

Dictionaries can also provide helpful information about the history of a word and reinforce the interrelationships among words in the same meaning "families." For example, a discussion of run-on entries illustrates how one word's entry can include information about related words—the entry for entrap also includes entraps and entrapment. The usage notes in dictionaries often explain subtle but important differences among words—usually the appropriateness of one word over another in a particular context. Words for which the dictionary is essential may be entered in a student's vocabulary notebook. Dictionaries can also contribute to an interest in and attitudes toward words that teachers and the students explore.

The usage notes in dictionaries reflect a powerful and consistent research finding: every word/concept we know, and the degree to which we really know it, depends on the relationship of that word/concept to other words/concepts. The thesaurus, another resource for word learning, also helps learners make fine distinctions among concepts and words. This differentiation of learners' conceptual domains is the essence of vocabulary development and growth.

11.2.6. Wide Reading

The importance of wide reading in the growth of students' vocabulary is critical. Given the staggering number of new words that children must add to their vocabularies each year, it would be impossible to directly teach all of them; it would require teaching about twenty new words a day each day of the school year. Through wide independent reading, students come in contact with vocabulary that rarely occurs in spoken language but that is much more likely to be encountered in printed language.

11.2.7. Create a Keen Awareness in Language and Words

Some children enter school with many more language skills than others. It seems reasonable to suggest that they also come with varying degrees of interest in words. Therefore, it is important that every teacher attempt to develop such an interest. It seems important that every teacher be interested in words themselves. Students' interest and curiosity about words are also stimulated when they learn the logic behind word origins and the many stories that underlie how words came about and came to mean what they do.

11.3. Teaching Vocabulary in Class

11.3.1. Focus on Vocabulary

Give vocabulary a high profile in the syllabus and the classroom so that students can see its importance and understand that learning a language isn't just about learning grammar. One of the first vocabulary learning strategies for any classroom is how to ask for words you don't know in English, and how to ask the meaning of English words you don't understand, so phrases like "What's the word for in English?," "How do you say ?," and "What does mean?" are useful to teach at the basic levels. As students progress, another useful strategy they can use is to paraphrase: "It's a kind of ," "It's like a ," and "It's for -ing X" etc. Focusing on these strategies puts vocabulary learning firmly on the classroom agenda.

Teachers can help learners get into the habit of noticing by making clear in classroom instruction and homework assignments: which items should be learned, what each item is (a single word, a phrase, a collocation etc.) and for what purpose (active use or passive recognition). And materials can help teachers in this in the following ways:

- Providing clearly marked vocabulary lessons
- Making the target vocabulary set stand out, including focused practice and regular review

11.3.2. Offer Variety

Teachers can use different ways to present vocabulary including pictures, sounds, and different text types with which students can identify: stories, conversations, web pages, questionnaires, news reports, etc. In each of these contexts, topics should be relevant to students' interests. Similarly, practice activities should vary and engage students at different levels. These should range from simple listen-and-repeat type of practice through controlled practice to opportunities to use the vocabulary in meaningful, personalised ways. Offering variety also means catering to different learning styles, and some students may use different learning styles for different types of language or in different learning situations. So this means offering activities that sometimes appeal to learners who are more "studial" and "analytic" (those who need to analyse the language and to be accurate in their use of it) as well as learners who are "experiential" and "global" (those who are less concerned with accuracy as with learning whole chunks of language) and catering to students who prefer to learn either by seeing, hearing, or doing something.

11.3.3. Repeat and Recycle

Learning vocabulary is largely about remembering, and students generally need to see, say, and write newly learned words many times before they can be said to have learned them. Some researchers have suggested various numbers of encounters with a word for learning to take place, ranging from five to up to twenty. Some suggest that an impressive amount of learning can take place when students learn lists of paired items; others suggest that this method of learning does not aid deeper understanding of the words or help develop fluency. However, most agree that repetition is an important aid to learning and that having to actively recall or "retrieve" a word is a more effective way of learning than simple exposure or just seeing a word over and over. Researchers also agree that repeating words aloud helps students remember words better than repeating them silently.

11.3.4. Organising Vocabulary

Organising vocabulary in meaningful ways makes it easier to learn. Textbooks often present new vocabulary in thematic sets as an aid to memory, but there are other types of organisation and these can be described under three broad headings: real-world groups, language-based groups, and personalised groups, examples of which are given below.

- Real-world groups occur in the real world, such as the countries within each continent, parts of the body, the foods in each food type (carbohydrate, protein, fats, etc.), activities that take place for a celebration (e.g., at a wedding), expressions people typically use in everyday situations (e.g., when someone passes an examination, has bad luck, etc.). Students can draw on their general knowledge to group English vocabulary according to concepts with which they are already familiar.
- Language-based groups draw on linguistic criteria as ways of grouping, for example, the different parts of speech of a word family; words that have the same prefix or suffix, or the same sound; verbs and dependent prepositions; collocations of different kinds (verb + noun; adjective + noun, etc.).
- Personalised groups use students' own preferences and experiences as the basis for the groups. It might include grouping vocabulary according to likes and dislikes, personal habits or personal history, for example, foods that you like and don't like, or eat often, sometimes, rarely, or that you ate for breakfast, lunch, and dinner yesterday. Making vocabulary personal helps to make it more memorable.

There are many different ways of practicing newly presented vocabulary in class, from repeating the words, controlled practice, or reacting to the content in some way, to using the vocabulary to say true things about oneself.

For example, in learning the vocabulary of countries, students can:

- Listen to the names of countries and repeat them
- Identify the countries they know in English, and add new ones
- Say which languages people speak in different countries
- Say which countries are near their own, or which they have personal connections with (I'm from . . . ; My brother lives in . . . , etc.), or which they would like to visit

At this point, a useful step is to take time to organise the new vocabulary in some way that allows students to "notice" and bring together the target words as the basis for a communicative activity or to have a clear record for review purposes, or both.

References

Anderson, R.C., and Freebody, P., "Vocabulary knowledge", In J. Guthrie (Ed.), *Comprehension and teaching: Research reviews,* Newark, DE: International Reading Association, 1981.

Bear, D.R., Ivernizzi, M., Templeton, S., and Johnston, F., *Words their way: Word study for phonics, vocabulary, and spelling instruction,* Upper Saddle River, NJ: Merrill/Prentice Hall, 2004.

Beck, I. L., McKeown, M. G., and Kucan, L., *Bringing words to life: Robust vocabulary instruction,* New York: Guilford, 2002.

Elley, W. B., "Vocabulary acquisition from listening to stories", *Reading Research Quarterly,* 1989.

Pikulski, J.J., and Chard, D.J., *Fluency: Bridge from decoding to reading comprehension,* Boston, MA: Houghton Mifflin Company, 2003.

Templeton, S., "Spelling", In J. Flood, D. Lapp, J. Squire, and J. M. Jensen (Eds.), *Handbook of research on teaching the English language arts* (2nd ed.), Mahwah, NY: Lawrence Erlbaum Associates, 2003.

_______________., "Teaching of spelling", In J. Guthrie (Senior Ed.), *Encyclopedia of education* (2nd ed.), New York: Macmillan, 2003.

_______________., "The vocabulary-spelling connection: Orthographic development and morphological knowledge at the intermediate grades and beyond", In J. Baumann and E. Kameenui (Eds.), *Vocabulary instruction,* New York: Guilford Press, 2004.

12

Assessment of Language Learning

Assessment can also help you to determine a learner's potential talent or capacity for learning languages. Also, it can help you to determine a student's proficiency in a language. Using assessment can also help to identify the strengths and weaknesses a learner has.

Some of the more popular forms of assessment that could be used with ESL students include dictation, cloze tests, multiple-choice tests, strip stories, role plays, writing samples, and portfolios.

1. Dictation is when a teacher reads a passage aloud and the students write what the teacher is saying.
2. Cloze tests are passages in which every nth word (ex. fifth, sixth, etc) is deleted and a blank is inserted in its place. The student must decide the appropriate words for the blanks.
3. Multiple-choice tests can be used the same way for ESL students that they are in the regular classroom.
4. Strip stories are passages that are cut apart sentence by sentence for the ESL students to put back in the correct order.
5. Role plays allow the ESL learners to be put in realistic situations and act them out in English.
6. Using writing samples helps teachers to determine certain grammatical strengths and weaknesses.
7. Portfolios are collections of your students' work which show their progress and achievements in one or more areas. Portfolios help students to see the growth that they have experienced in their language development.

One of the most challenging tasks for language instructors is finding effective ways to determine what and how much their students are actually learning. Instructors need to think carefully about what kinds of knowledge their tests allow students to demonstrate.

12.1. Traditional Tests

Traditional pencil-and-paper tests ask students to read or listen to a selection and then answer questions about it, or to choose or produce a correct grammatical form or vocabulary item. Such tests can be helpful as measures of students' knowledge of language forms and their listening and reading comprehension ability. However, instructors need to consider whether these tests are accurate reflections of authentic language use. The tests usually do not present reading comprehension and listening comprehension questions until after students have read or listened to the selection. In real life, however, people know what information they are seeking before they read or listen. That is, they have specific information gaps in mind as they begin, and those gaps define the purpose for reading or listening.

To make language tests more like authentic listening and reading activities, instructors can give students the comprehension questions before they listen to or read the selection. This procedure sets up the information gaps that students will then seek to fill as they listen or read. Instructors also need to be careful about what pencil-and-paper tests are actually testing.

A quiz on which students listen to a selection and then respond to written questions is testing reading ability as well as listening skills and will give a lower-than-appropriate score for students whose oral comprehension is stronger than their reading comprehension. A test on which students read a selection and then answer multiple-choice questions is testing their knowledge of the language used in the questions as well as that used in the selection itself. If the language used in the questions is not keyed to students' proficiency level, the test will not reflect their ability accurately.

Language instructors also encounter students who do well on pencil-and-paper tests of grammar and sentence structure, but make mistakes when using the same forms in oral interaction. In such cases, the test is indicating what students know *about* the language, but is not providing an accurate measure of what they are able to actually *do* with it. When the goal of language instruction is the development of communicative competence, instructors can supplement (or, in some cases, replace) traditional tests with alternative assessment methods that provide more accurate measures of progress toward communication proficiency goals. This can be done by combining formative and summative types of assessment.

12.1.1. Productive and Receptive Tests

The tests may be of a productive nature where students are asked to produce—speak, read aloud, write—utterances, or perform tasks. These may be of a receptive nature where students are asked to read silently and answer multiple choice questions, which demand correct recognition rather than the production of the answer.

12.1.2. Vocabulary Tests

Vocabulary tests are of several kinds. Beginner's vocabulary skill is tested through questions which expect a yes or no answer, or by asking them to perform a simple task. In multiple choice questions, "a sentence with a missing word is presented; students choose one of four vocabulary items given to complete the sentence. A third type, multiple choice paraphrase, is a test in which a sentence with one word underlined is given. Students choose which of four words is the closest in meaning to the underlined item. A fourth kind of test, simple completion (words), has students write in the missing part of words that appear in sentences".

Synonyms and antonyms may also be elicited. Testing the knowledge and use of subtle shades of meanings reflected in words somewhat synonymous is another useful test. Asking the students to use words in appropriate sentences is another exercise which has been traditionally used in language textbooks.

12.1.3. Grammar Tests

Limited response questions which ask students to perform certain tasks, multiple choice completion, simple completion of sentences, and cloze test are some of the test forms used in the grammar section. The grammatical structures offer an endless list of test items.

12.1.4. Pronunciation Tests

Pronunciation tests focus on effective communication, not on perfect pronunciation. Pronunciation of individual sounds, phrases, or sentences is not any more highlighted. Oral repetition, multiple choice hearing identification, reading aloud, simple dialogues, and simple narrations are very useful forms to test the pronunciation skill.

12.1.5. Reading Tests

Reading tests range from reading aloud to reading comprehension. Students in the beginning levels need to be tested as to their ability to "read" the words, phrases, and sentences with appropriate pronunciation and sentence melody. This requires the mastery of the letter-sound correspondence and other phonological rules such as vowel reduction, placement of stress, and use of appropriate syllabic pauses. Reading comprehension, reading speed, and skimming techniques are other items of importance to be covered in reading tests.

12.1.6. Writing Tests

Sentence combining, sentence expansion, sentence reduction, copying, and dictation are often used in the beginning level tests in writing. Guided writing and changing the passage are also popular test forms.

12.1.7. Listening Tests

Picture cues have been found very effective in testing listening skill. You should test your students only in forms that are familiar to them. Do not introduce new test forms during testing. However, you may combine several situations already familiar to your students and create new ones from out of the familiar contexts. Do not introduce new vocabulary or idioms or new structures in your tests. Keep your tests brief and focused upon specific language skills.

12.2. Alternative Assessment

Many educators have come to recognise that alternative assessments are an important means of gaining a dynamic picture of students' academic and linguistic development. Alternative assessment refers to procedures and techniques which can be used within the context of instruction and can be easily incorporated into the daily activities of the school or classroom. It is particularly useful with English as a second language students because it employs strategies that ask students to show what they can do. Although there is no single definition of alternative assessment, the main goal is to "gather evidence about how students are approaching, processing, and completing real-life tasks in a particular domain". Alternative assessments generally meet the following criteria:

- Focus is on documenting individual student growth over time, rather than comparing students with one another.
- Emphasis is on students' strengths (what they know), rather than weaknesses (what they don't know).
- Consideration is given to the learning styles, language proficiencies, cultural and educational backgrounds, and grade levels of students.

Alternative assessment includes a variety of measures that can be adapted for different situations.

Alternative assessment uses activities that reveal what students can do with language, emphasizing their strengths instead of their weaknesses. Alternative assessment instruments are not only designed and structured differently from traditional tests, but are also graded or scored differently. Because alternative assessment is performance based, it helps instructors emphasize that the point of language learning is communication for meaningful purposes.

Alternative assessment methods work well in learner-centered classrooms because they are based on the idea that students can evaluate their own learning and learn from the evaluation process. These methods give learners opportunities to reflect on both their linguistic development and their learning processes (what helps them learn and what might help them learn better). Alternative assessment thus gives instructors a way to connect assessment with review of learning strategies.

The following are the features of alternative assessment:

- Assessment is based on authentic tasks that demonstrate learners' ability to accomplish communication goals
- Instructor and learners focus on communication, not on right and wrong answers
- Learners help to set the criteria for successful completion of communication tasks
- Learners have opportunities to assess themselves and their peers

With alternative assessment, students are expected to participate actively in evaluating themselves and one another. Learners who are used to traditional teacher-centered classrooms have not been expected to take responsibility for assessment before and may need time to adjust to this new role. They also may be skeptical that peers can provide them with feedback that will enhance their learning.

Instructors need to prepare students for the use of alternative assessments and allow time to teach them how to use them, so that alternative assessment will make an effective contribution to the learning process.

- Introduce alternative assessment gradually while continuing to use more traditional forms of assessment. Begin by using checklists and rubrics yourself; move to self and peer evaluation later.
- Create a supportive classroom environment in which students feel comfortable with one another.
- Explain the rationale for alternative assessment.
- Engage students in a discussion of assessment. Elicit their thoughts on the values and limitations of traditional forms of assessment and help them see ways that alternative assessment can enhance evaluation of what learners can do with language.
- Give students guidance on how to reflect on and evaluate their own performance and that of others.

12.2.1. Alternative Assessment Methods

Effective alternative assessment relies on observations that are recorded using checklists and rubrics.

12.2.1.1. Checklists

Checklists are often used for observing performance in order to keep track of a student's progress or work over time. They can also be used to determine whether students have met established criteria on a task. To construct a checklist, identify the different parts of a specific communication task and any other requirements associated with it. Create a list of these with columns for marking *yes* and *no*.

Checklists can be useful for classroom assessment because they are easy to construct and use, and they align closely with tasks. At the same time, they are limited in that they do not provide an assessment of the relative quality of a student's performance on a particular task.

12.2.1.2. Rubrics

Rubrics are primarily used for language tasks that involve some kind of oral or written production on the part of the student. It is possible to create a generic rubric that can be used with multiple speaking or writing tasks, but assessment is more accurate when the instructor uses rubrics that are fitted to the task and the goals of instruction. There are four main types of rubrics.

Holistic rubrics

Holistic scales or rubrics respond to language performance as a *whole*. Each score on a holistic scale represents an overall impression; one integrated score is assigned to a performance. The emphasis in holistic scoring is on what a student does well. Holistic rubrics commonly have four or six points. The popup window shows a sample four-point holistic scale created for the purposes of assessing writing performance. Holistic scoring is primarily used for large-scale assessment when a relatively quick yet consistent approach to scoring is necessary. It is less useful for classroom purposes because it provides little information to students about their performance.

Analytic rubrics

Analytic scales are divided into separate categories representing different aspects or dimensions of performance. For example, dimensions for writing performance might include content, organisation, vocabulary, grammar, and mechanics. Each dimension is scored separately, then dimension scores are added to determine an overall score. Analytic rubrics have two advantages:

- The instructor can give different weights to different dimensions. This allows the instructor to give more credit for dimensions that are more important to the overall success of the communication task. For example, in a writing rubric, the dimension of content might have a total point range of 30, whereas the range for mechanics might be only 10.
- They provide more information to students about the strengths and weaknesses of various aspects of their language performance.

However, analytic scoring has also been criticised because the parts do not necessarily add up to the whole. Providing separate scores for different dimensions of a student's writing or speaking performance does not give the teacher or the student a good assessment of the whole of a performance.

Primary trait rubrics

In primary trait scoring, the instructor predetermines the main criterion or primary trait for successful performance of a task. This approach thus involves narrowing the criteria for judging performance to one main dimension.

Multitrait rubrics

The multitrait approach is similar to the primary trait approach but allows for rating performance on three or four dimensions rather than just one. Multitrait rubrics resemble analytic rubrics in that several aspects are scored individually. However, where an analytic scale includes traditional dimensions such as content, organisation, and grammar, a multitrait rubric involves dimensions that are more closely aligned with features of the task.

12.3. Performance-based Assessments

Performance-based assessments include interviews, oral reports, role plays, describing, explaining, summarising, retelling, paraphrasing stories or text material, and so on. Oral assessments should be conducted on an ongoing basis to monitor comprehension and thinking skills. When conducting interviews in English with students in the early stages of language development to determine English proficiency and content knowledge, teachers are advised to use visual cues as much as possible and allow for a minimal amount of English in the responses.

Role plays can be used across the curriculum with all grade levels and with any number of people. For example, a teacher can take on the role of a character who knows less than the students about a particular subject area. Students are motivated to convey facts or information prompted by questions from the character. This is a fun-filled way for a teacher to conduct informal assessments of students' knowledge in any subject.

Teachers can also ask students to use role play to express mathematical concepts. For example, a group of students can become a numerator, a denominator, a fraction line, a proper fraction, an improper fraction, and an equivalent fraction. Speaking in the first person, students can introduce themselves and their functions in relationship to one another. Role plays can also be used in science to demonstrate concepts such as the life cycle. Role plays can serve as an alternative to traditional book reports. Students can transform themselves into a character or object from the book.

12.3.1. Portfolios

Portfolios are used to collect samples of student work over time to track student development. The following types of materials can be included in a portfolio:

- Audio- and videotaped recordings of readings or oral presentations.
- Writing samples such as dialogue journal entries, book reports, writing assignments (drafts or final copies), reading log entries, or other writing projects.

- Art work such as pictures or drawings, and graphs and charts.
- Conference or interview notes and anecdotal records.
- Checklists (by teacher, peers, or student).
- Tests and quizzes.

To gain multiple perspectives on students' academic development, it is important for teachers to include more than one type of material in the portfolio.

12.4. Peer Assessment

One of the ways in which students internalise the characteristics of quality work is by evaluating the work of their peers. However, if they are to offer helpful feedback, students must have a clear understanding of what they are to look for in their peers' work. The instructor must explain expectations clearly to them before they begin.

One way to make sure students understand this type of evaluation is to give students a practice session with it. The instructor provides a sample writing or speaking assignment. As a group, students determine what should be assessed and how criteria for successful completion of the communication task should be defined. Then the instructor gives students a sample completed assignment. Students assess this using the criteria they have developed, and determine how to convey feedback clearly to the fictitious student.

Students can also benefit from using rubrics or checklists to guide their assessments. At first these can be provided by the instructor; once the students have more experience, they can develop them themselves. An example of a peer editing checklist for a writing assignment is given in the popup window. Notice that the checklist asks the peer evaluator to comment primarily on the content and organisation of the essay. It helps the peer evaluator focus on these areas by asking questions about specific points, such as the presence of examples to support the ideas discussed.

For peer evaluation to work effectively, the learning environment in the classroom must be supportive. Students must feel comfortable and trust one another in order to provide honest and constructive feedback. Instructors who use group work and peer assessment frequently can help students develop trust by forming them into small groups early in the semester and having them work in the same groups throughout the term. This allows them to become more comfortable with each other and leads to better peer feedback.

12.5. Self Assessment

Students can become better language learners when they engage in deliberate thought about what they are learning and how they are learning it. In this kind of reflection, students step back from the learning process to think about their language learning strategies and their progress as language learners. Such self assessment encourages students to become independent learners and can increase their motivation.

The successful use of student self assessment depends on three key elements:

- Goal setting
- Guided practice with assessment tools
- Portfolios

12.5.1. Goal Setting

Goal setting is essential because students can evaluate their progress more clearly when they have targets against which to measure their performance. In addition, students' motivation to learn increases when they have self-defined, and therefore relevant, learning goals.

At first, students tend to create lofty long-range goals ("to speak Russian)" that do not lend themselves to self assessment. To help students develop realistic, short-term, attainable goals, instructors can use a framework like SMART goals outline shown in the popup window.

One way to begin the process of introducing students to self-assessment is to create student-teacher contracts. Contracts are written agreements between students and instructors, which commonly involve determining the number and type of assignments that are required for particular grades. For example, a student may agree to work toward the grade of "B" by completing a specific number of assignments at a level of quality described by the instructor. Contracts can serve as a good way of helping students to begin to consider establishing goals for themselves as language learners.

12.5.2. Guided Practice with Assessment Tools

Students do not learn to monitor or assess their learning on their own; they need to be taught strategies for self monitoring and self assessment. Techniques for teaching students these strategies are parallel to those used for teaching learning strategies. The instructor models the technique (use of a checklist or rubric, for example); students then try the technique themselves; finally, students discuss whether and how well the technique worked and what to do differently next time.

In addition to checklists and rubrics for specific communication tasks, students can also use broader self-assessment tools to reflect on topics they have studied, skills they have learned, their study habits, and their sense of their overall strengths and weaknesses. An example of such a tool appears in the popup window.

Students can share their self-assessments with a peer or in a small group, with instructions that they compare their impressions with other criteria such as test scores, teacher evaluations, and peers' opinions. This kind of practice helps students to be aware of their learning. It also informs the teacher about students' thoughts on their progress, and gives the teacher feedback about course content and instruction.

12.5.3. Portfolios

Portfolios are purposeful, organised, systematic collections of student work that tell the story of a student's efforts, progress, and achievement in specific areas. The student participates in the selection of portfolio content, the development of guidelines for selection, and the definition of criteria for judging merit. Portfolio assessment is a joint process for instructor and student.

Portfolio assessment emphasizes evaluation of students' progress, processes, and performance over time. There are two basic types of portfolios:

— A process portfolio serves the purpose of classroom-level assessment on the part of both the instructor and the student. It most often reflects formative assessment, although it may be assigned a grade at the end of the semester or academic year. It may also include summative types of assignments that were awarded grades.

— A product portfolio is more summative in nature. It is intended for a major evaluation of some sort and is often accompanied by an oral presentation of its contents. For example, it may be used as a evaluation tool for graduation from a programme or for the purpose of seeking employment.

In both types of portfolios, emphasis is placed on including a variety of tasks that elicit spontaneous as well as planned language performance for a variety of purposes and audiences, using rubrics to assess performance, and demonstrating reflection about learning, including goal setting and self and peer assessment.

References

Bachman, L. F., *Fundamental considerations in language testing,* London: Oxford, 1990.

Bailey, K., Freeman, D., & Curtis, A., "Goals-based evaluation procedures: How students perceive what teachers intend", *TESOL Journal,* 2001.

Baron, J. B., "SEA Usage of Alternative Assessment: The Connecticut Experience", *ERIC Document Reproduction Service No. ED 349 816,* 1991.

Cohen, A. D., *Assessing language ability in the classroom* (2nd ed.), Boston, MA: Heinle & Heinle, 1994.

Evansville-Vanderburgh School Corp., "Portfolio assessment in foreign language, pilot project", *ERIC Document Reproduction Services No. ED 368 197,* 1993.

Fraser, Catherine, "Portfolio assessment in the foreign language classroom: What works", In G. K. Crouse (Ed.), *Report of Central States Conference on the Teaching of Foreign Languages: Broadening the frontiers of foreign language education,* Lincolnwood, IL: National Textbook Co., 1995.

Hancock, C. R., "Alternative assessment and second language study: What and why?", *ERIC Digest,* July, 1994.

_______________ (Ed.), "Teaching, testing, and assessing: Making the connection", *Northeast Conference Reports,* Lincolnwood, IL: National Textbook Co., 1994.

Hart, D., "Authentic assessment: A handbook for educators", *Reading,* MA: Addison-Wesley, 1994.

Shohamy, E., *A practical handbook in language testing for the second language teacher,* Israel: Shoshana Goldberg, 1985.

Valette, R. M., *Modern language testing,* New York: Harcourt Brace Jovanovich, 1977.

Wiggins, G., *A true test: Toward more authentic and equitable assessment,* Phi Delta Kappan, May 1989.

_______________ ., "Toward more authentic assessment of language performance", In C. R. Hancock (Ed.), *Teaching, testing, and assessment. Making the connection,* Northeast Conference Reports, Lincolnwood, IL: National Textbook Company, 1994.

Bibliography

Asher, James, *Learning Another Language Through Actions: The Complete Teacher's Guidebook,* Los Gatos, CA: Sly Oaks Productions, 1977.

Asher, J., "Motivating children and adults to acquire a second language", In J.W. Oller, Jr., and P.A. Richard-Amato (eds.) *Methods that work: A smorgasbord of ideas for language teachers,* Rowley, MA: Newbury House Publishers, Inc., 1983.

Avery, P.- Ehrlich, S. (Eds.), *The Teaching of Pronunciation: An Introduction for Teachers of English as a Second Language,* Oxford: Oxford University Press, 1987.

Baugh, Albert C., Thomas Cable, *A history of the English language,* 5th ed., Routledge, 2002.

Bragg, Melvyn, *The Adventure of English: The Biography of a Language,* Arcade Publishing, 2004.

Brown, A. (Ed.), *Teaching English Pronunciation,* A Book of Readings, London: Routledge, 1991.

Brown, and G. Yule, *Teaching the spoken language,* New York: Cambridge University Press, 1983.

Brown, H. Douglas, *Teaching by Principles: An Interactive Approach to Language Pedagogy,* Prentice Hall, 1994.

_______________ ., "The role of listening comprehension: A theoretical base", *Foreign Language Annals,* 1984.

Bondy, E., "Children's definitions of reading: Products of an interactive process", *Paper presented at the annual meeting of the American Educational Research Association,* Chicago, Illinois, 1985.

Bygate, M., Tonkyn, A., & Williams, E. (Eds.), *Grammar and the language teacher,* Hemel Hempstead, England: Prentice Hall, 1994.

Byrd, P., "Writing grammar textbooks: Theory and practice", *System,* 1994.

Canning, C., "Visual Perception and Language Learning", *TESOL Arabia News,* 6:1, November 1998.

Celce-Murcia, M., & Hilles, S., *Techniques and resources in teaching grammar,* Oxford: Oxford University Press, 1988.

Celce-Murcia, M, Brinton, D, Goodwin, J., *Teaching pronunciation: A reference for teachers of English to speakers of other languages,* New York: Cambridge University Press, 1996.

Chapelle C., *Computer applications in second language acquisition: foundations for teaching, testing and research,* Cambridge: Cambridge University Press, 2001.

Crystal, David, *The Cambridge encyclopedia of the English language,* 2nd ed., Cambridge University Press, 2003.

Crandall, J., Spanos, G., Christian, D., Simich-Dudgeon, C., and Willetts, K., "Integrating language and content instruction for language minority students", Silver Spring, MD: National Clearinghouse for Bilingual Education, 1987.

Dalton, C, Seidlhofer, B., *Pronunciation,* Oxford: Oxford University Press, 1994.

de Szendeffy J., *A practical guide to using computers in language teaching,* Ann Arbor: University of Michigan Press, 2005.

Finocchiaro, Mary & Brumfit, Christopher, *The Functional-Notional Approach: From Theory to Practice,* Oxford University Press, 1983.

Fraser, H., *Teaching Pronunciation: A handbook for teachers and trainers,* Sydney: TAFE Access Division (funded by the Adult Literacy Project through the Commonwealth of Australia Department of Education Training and Youth Affairs), 2001.

Flores, B. and Garcia, E.A., "A collaborative learning and teaching experience using journal writing", *NABE Journal,* 1984.

Goodman, K., *What's whole in whole language,* Portsmouth, NH: Heinemann, 1986.

Goodman, K., Goodman, Y., and Hood, W.J., *The whole language evaluation book,* Portsmouth, NH: Heinemann, 1989.

Halliday, MAK, *An introduction to functional grammar,* 2nd ed., London: Edward Arnold, 1994.

Hayford, Harrison; Howard P. Vincent, *Reader and Writer,* Houghton Mifflin Company, 1954.

Haycraft, B., *The Teaching of Pronunciation: A Classroom guide,* London: Longman, 1971.

Harmer, J., *The practice of English language teaching,* London: Longman, 1991.

Hamayan, E. and Pfleger, M., "Developing literacy in English as a second language: Guidelines for teachers of young children from non-literate backgrounds", Silver Spring, MD: National Clearinghouse for Bilingual Education, 1987.

Jarvis H., "Technology and change in English Language Teaching (ELT)", *The Asian EFL Journal,* 2005.

Kenworthy, J., *Teaching English Pronunciation,* London: Longman, 1987.

Kramsch, C., *Context and culture in language teaching,* New York: Oxford University Press, 1993.

Krashen, Stephen D., & Terrell, Tracy D., *The Natural Approach: Language Acquisition in the Classroom,* Pergamon Press, 1983.

Laroy, C., *Pronunciation,* Oxford: Oxford University Press, 1995.

Larsen-Freeman, Dianne, *Techniques and Principles in Language Teaching,* New York: Oxford University Press, 1986.

Lightbown, P., & Spada, N., *How languages are learned,* Oxford: Oxford University Press, 1992.

Lund, R.J., "A taxonomy for teaching second language listening", *Foreign Language Annals,* 1990.

Larsen-Freeman, D., "Teaching grammar", In M. Celce-Murcia (Ed.), *Teaching English as a second or foreign language,* (3rd ed.), Boston: Heinle & Heinle, 2001.

Larsen-Freeman, D., *Teaching language: From grammar to grammaring,* Boston: Heinle & Heinle, 2001.

McArthur, T. (ed.), *The Oxford Companion to the English Language,* Oxford University Press, 1992.

Mendelsohn, D.J., & Rubin, J., *A guide for the teaching of second language listening,* San Diego, CA: Dominie Press, 1995.

Morley, J., "Listening comprehension in second/foreign language instruction", In M. Celce-Murcia (Ed.), *Teaching English as a second or foreign language,* Boston, MA: Heinle & Heinle, 1991.

Mitchell, R; F. Myles, *Second Language Learning Theories,* London: Arnold, 1998.

Nunan, David, *Language Teaching Methodology: A Textbook for Teachers,* Prentice Hall, 1991.

Nunan, D., & Miller, L.(Eds.), *New ways in teaching listening,* Alexandria, VA: TESOL, 1995.

Omaggio-Hadley, A., *Teaching language in context (2nd ed.),* Boston, MA: Heinle & Heinle, 1993.

Oxford, R., & Cohen, A., "Language learning strategies: Critical issues of concept and classification", *Applied Language Learning,* 1992.

Prator, Clifford H. & Celce-Murcia, Marianne, "An outline of language teaching approaches", In Celce-Murcia, Marianne & McIntosh, Lois (Ed.), *Teaching English as a Second or Foreign Language,* Newbury House, 1979.

Ravichandran, T., *Computer-assisted language learning (CALL) in the perspective of the interactive approach: Advantages and apprehensions,* 2000.

Richards, Jack & Rodgers, Theodore, *Approaches and Methods in Language Teaching,* New York: Cambridge University Press, 1986.

Richards, J.C., "Listening comprehension: Approach, design, procedure", *TESOL Quarterly,* 1983.

Robinson, Orrin, *Old English and Its Closest Relatives,* Stanford Univ. Press, 1992.

Rost, M., *Listening in language learning,* London: Longman, 1990.

Rubin, J., "The contribution of video to the development of competence in listening", In D.J. Mendelsohn & J. Rubin (Eds.), *A guide for the teaching of second language listening,* San Diego, CA: Dominie Press, 1995.

Schön, D., *The reflective practitioner: How professionals think in action,* New York: Basic Books, 1983.

Seldin, P., *The teaching portfolio: A practical guide to improved performance and promotion/tenure decisions,* Bolton, MA: Anker Publishing, 1991.

Son J.-B. (ed.), *Computer Assisted Language Learning: concepts, contexts and practices,* Lincoln, NE: iUniverse, 2004.

Scarcella, R.C.- Oxford, R.L., "Second language pronunciation: state of the art in instruction", *System* 22, 1994.

Setter, J.- Jenkins, J., "Pronunciation", *Language Teaching,* 2005.

Staton, J., Kreeft, J., and Gutstein, S., *Dialogue journals as a reading event,* Dialogue, 1985.

Traynor, Patrick, "Effects of computer-assisted instruction on different learners", *Journal of Instructional Psychology,* July 2003.

Underwood, M., *Teaching listening,* London: Longman, 1989.

Ueland, B., *If you want to write,* Saint Paul, MN: Graywolf Press, 1987.

Warschauer Mark, *Computer Assisted Language Learning: an Introduction,* 2008.

Wallace, M. J., *Training foreign language teachers: A reflective approach,* New York: Cambridge University Press, 1991.

Index